The Revd Eric Fisher was born in Stoke-on-Trent, England, in 1930. A graduate of Birmingham University, his first job was with the Colonial Service in Sierra Leone, where he rose to the rank of Provincial Commissioner. On his return, after a short period working for National Savings, he began training for the Anglican ministry at the College of the Resurrection, Mirfield, was ordained in 1972 and priested in 1973. He has been curate of Styvechale, Coventry (1972–75) and All Saints, Chesterfield (1975–78); team vicar of Buxton and chaplain of its hospitals (1978–84); rector of Shirland (1984–89). Since 1989 he has been vicar of St Matthew's, Sheffield.

HEALING MIRACLES

Eric Fisher

Fount

An Imprint of HarperCollins*Publishers*

Fount Paperbacks is an Imprint of
HarperCollins*Religious*,
Part of HarperCollins*Publishers*
77–85 Fulham Palace Road
Hammersmith, London W6 8JB

First published in Great Britain
in 1993 by Fount Paperbacks

1 3 5 7 9 10 8 6 4 2

A catalogue record for this book is
available from the British Library

ISBN 0 00 627657 1

Printed and bound in Great Britain by
HarperCollinsManufacturing Glasgow

CONTENTS

Chapter One

THE POWER
AND THE GLORY

The Alice Jones affair was really two miracles —
not one.

First there was the actual healing itself which
has defied all rational explanation. Second there
was the amazing explosion of interest caused by
the BBC TV programme which reported it, and
the avalanche of enquiries that followed.

The contrast to the many quiet manifestations
of the Healing Ministry observed in the previous
ten years or so of my work couldn't have been
more pronounced.

In this book I want to record some of the
experiences I have had in this ministry, and also
to describe some of the work of the many other
people likewise involved. I hope that you might
be challenged to seek out or recommit yourself to
Jesus, whose power alone makes this work
possible. No one seeks Him in vain.

This combination of healing and preaching is
causing tidal waves of conversions to Christ

throughout the world at a rate of thousands per day, more even, it is said, than in the first century.

If the Charismatic or Pentecostalist movements, often associated with these advances, are not to everybody's liking, you have little to fear. My earliest encouragement came from two Anglican bishops, the Bishop of Coventry and Bishop Bardsley, the Bishop of Chester, who was himself one of my patients. The incoming tide is lapping at the doors of our more conventional churches and we must all be ready to grasp the opportunity He is offering us. It is of greater consequence than the healing of a few people here and there, important as that may be to the individuals concerned. It could be the key to a new Christian era.

Before I begin, I would like to make my position clear in two respects. First, I believe that Jesus Christ is the only ultimate healer, whether through doctors, nurses and hospitals or by the practices of what we call the Healing Ministry, which includes prayer and the laying on of hands.

Second, we carry out this ministry in response to His directive, recorded in the gospels, to preach and heal. Let there be no cries of "witchcraft".

When Jesus walked the earth He had only three years at the most to create such an impact that the value systems of the human race would be corrected and established for all time — a daunting task for an obscure craftsman in a little-known province of the Roman Empire.

He achieved it by healing people singly and in large numbers. It was the unanswerable confirmation of His message, and Jesus made sure that the message was left with those who experienced His healing touch.

The situation is much the same today. Then, as now, the healing of broken bodies is good, but it is the message, the healing of hearts and minds, that is the really important objective. Sooner or later our bodies will die but, we believe, the essential person will continue to survive in some closer relationship to this Jesus.

But back to the case of Alice Jones. I had gone on a mission to Haydock, near Liverpool, in 1980, where the vicar had asked me to visit certain people on his sick list, including Alice Jones. A mission, in this sense, was an exercise where a team of perhaps eight people is sent out round the houses in the parish to teach and preach.

Alice was about forty years of age. She had been a teacher at the local school, next to the church. She had been doing dinner duty and, while lifting some tables, had fallen and hurt her hip. As a result she had been bothered with pain in her back for seven years, and before I met her had undergone a serious operation known as a spinal fusion. It had involved taking a piece of bone out of her hip and grafting it on to her spine. Six people had undergone this operation and all but Alice were confined to wheelchairs. She could walk with great difficulty, using a calliper which lifted her left foot slightly off the ground. She was only able to control the pain by an excessive use of drugs and alcohol and, in her view, was on the way to becoming an alcoholic, like some others who had also had this operation. She had been assessed, by the State, as one hundred per cent disabled.

I found Alice to be a typical middle-aged school teacher living with her husband, Frank, in a nice bungalow near the middle of Haydock town. On my first visit she was very weepy, depressed and in a bitter frame of mind. She had lost all sensation in her left leg, the foot was twisted right over to one side, and her spine was out of true.

Before I go any further I have to tell you of my brother in the Spirit, an Italian Capuchin monk called Padre Pio who had an amazing gift of healing. He was the only priest in the history of the Catholic Church to bear in his body the Stigmata – the wounds of Christ.

Padre Pio died in 1968 but, in my view, continues to heal. In fact, he said that after his death he would work more in Heaven than he had on Earth. I have been aware of his assistance on many occasions.

Before visiting Alice I said a special prayer to

Padre Pio from his "Novena" or prayer card, and asked for his protection and support. I had also distributed these cards in the church after early morning Mass. They show a picture of Padre Pio and give an account of his life of service and austerity.

I began by saying a prayer for Alice and all the sick of the parish, and laid my hands on her back, running them up and down her spine. She cried out that she felt a warm glow flowing down her spine and all over. This was surprising to her because, since the accident, her back had always felt icy cold. I continued to minister for about fifteen minutes, then stopped. We agreed that I would return the next day at about the same time.

I did not know why I had stopped at the time but now I have no doubt that it was Padre Pio protecting me. I felt that if I had employed any great pressure on the spine it might have adversely affected the spinal fusion.

During the service in church that night I asked Padre Pio for a miracle.

The next day I returned to Alice's home. She seemed to be less aggressive and less bitter but she showed no particular optimism or expectation. After starting again on the spine, I began to treat her bad left leg. It seemed to me that there had been hardly any wastage of the calf muscles, so I was surprised that she had no sensation. She shouted out that she could feel "pins and needles" in her leg and that it was all hot. Gradually these sensations embraced the whole of the limb, through the ankle to the twisted foot. I concentrated the healing there, gradually straightening it out and getting it to sit firmly on the floor. I felt the muscles and tendons yielding. The foot straightened right out and rested flat on the floor. Incredibly these changes did not activate intense pain, although the operated portion of the spine must have been affected.

I told her to get up and walk. "I can't walk," she said, but I kept urging her to try. After what seemed to be an eternity she raised herself and started to hobble across the room sobbing with joy. There was the deep silence in the room which I have only experienced on the rare occasions when something tremendous is happening.

Later that night Alice told me of something which, unknown to me, was happening to her during the healing. She said that when she looked down on me she saw, superimposed on my face, the face of an older man with a beard. She remembered closing her eyes and opening them again but this strange old man was still there. She could hear a voice commanding her to walk and the old fears of falling and failure returned to her. Then the word "walk" seemed to reverberate round and round in her head, and with it came a sense of confidence and faith. She walked round the room to the door and returned to her armchair. She was utterly amazed. The old man had gone. She saw me again and all her pain and discomfort had been removed.

Alice's daughter had been present at both healings. She said she had been aware of a strong smell of perfume and felt compelled to pick up her baby son, who had been having sleeping problems since birth, and stand with him behind her mother's chair. She had the sensation of being caught up in a warm comforting blanket.

When Alice's husband Frank returned home that night his wife ran down the drive to meet him. He could not believe his eyes. He is a qualified orthopaedic nurse and had been instrumental in persuading Alice to have the operation. Now he was worried in case her previous condition would return, a sad disappointment after all her suffering. In fact he was about to see a further miracle.

Every night Frank packed an ulcer in Alice's heel which had been caused by a drawing pin. This had produced a large hole which would not heal. That night he got out the bandages as usual but he warned Alice that dressing the wound was likely to be painful, now that feeling had been restored to her leg.

The ulcer had vanished.

At first he thought she had given him the wrong leg but there was no sign of the ulcer, not even a mark.

There still remained the mystery of the identity of the old man she had seen. It was soon to be solved. Frank and Alice attended the Healing Service in the church that night where Alice saw one of the cards bearing a picture of Padre Pio. Immediately she knew that this was the person she had seen in her living room that afternoon.

When the congregation saw Alice walk into church accompanied by Frank and their two daughters there were gasps of amazement. They all knew that Alice had been unable to walk for many months. There was no need for a sermon that night; a miracle had taken place in their parish.

Inevitably some people told Alice that the healing could not last or that it was a confidence trick of some sort. Her doctor said that her recovery was medically impossible. But he told her to tell her priest that he had performed a miracle and that he, a Jew, could confirm it.

Not only was there a physical change; Alice underwent a spiritual transformation as well. She began to pray again. She regained her faith and was to prove to be a veritable missionary in spreading the cause of Padre Pio all over England. Just to listen to Alice telling of her miraculous healing challenges our faith and our hope. It is hoped that Alice's healing will be included in the evidence now being collected for the proceedings relating to the possible beatification of Padre Pio.

I had the privilege of accompanying Alice and Frank to San Giovanni — Padre Pio's church — near Foggia in southern Italy, and watched the tears well up in the eyes of Padre Pio's Franciscan brothers as Alice told her story.

The ripples of interest spread ever outwards. A Polish lady read an account of it in a magazine and invited me to visit Portugal, where we had an extensive ministry in Lisbon and elsewhere. This was followed by a second ministry in May 1988. These trips are discussed in greater depth in later chapters.

Then I was asked to visit a Mrs Mary Murton, who had lost a child with leukemia, more as a counsellor rather than a healer. We became good friends.

Her son Paul happened to be an independent TV producer. He was asked by Scottish Television to do a film about miracles, and Mary suggested that he spoke to me. He and his co-producer, Ros Borland, met me at St Matthew's and we discussed the format of the film at some length. He did not claim any personal faith but as they left both of them, like Alice's daughter, scented the sudden perfume which is connected with Padre Pio.

The Alice Jones case is the kind of thing which does happen in the Healing Ministry, albeit rarely. I have known only a dozen or so such dramatic cases in my twenty years of this ministry, but the numbers of lesser blessings, of pain relieved, of faith restored, of healings of all kinds are many. Indeed it could be argued that if there was such a dramatic cure every day of the week it might be contrary to God's greater purpose.

Though He always seeks the best of everything for His people He will not trap anyone into being forced to believe. But more of that later too.

Chapter Two

BEGINNINGS

Most people of mature age and judgement could identify a few persons, seldom more than half a dozen, whose influence has significantly altered the course of their lives.

It was through one of these, a famous healer, Mary Rogers (a friend of the Bishop of Coventry, in whose diocese I was working at the time) that I first "met" Padre Pio. It occurred during 1972/3, when I used to visit Mary in her London home, to learn as much as I could about the Healing Ministry. I had already been advised by the Bishop that my role in the Church would be in the Healing Ministry rather than in parish work.

It was a minor miracle that I was in the Church at all. For much of my early life I was brought up by my father's sister, who was a keen member of an evangelistic Bethesda Chapel. It was in Sunday School that I first became aware of the living reality of Jesus Christ. I suppose I would be about the age of three and a half years, and ever since He has been a living companion to me, more real than any human being.

As a boy, on my way to Iona I had a vision of Him. I do not know where the place was except that I could stop and look out over a valley where there was a great rock, and the image of Jesus superimposed itself over that rock.

He looked about twelve years old, with very black curly hair, a rather dark complexion, and I particularly noticed His very Jewish nose. This vision was not an "interior" experience within my head but an "exterior" one. It was not until I went to Israel, many years later, that I was able to see Him "in the flesh", as it were, on the streets of Jerusalem, where there were many young boys who looked just like the vision I had had of Jesus.

I was a rather solitary child, mostly living in a world of my own, though I did grow up in the company of an older brother and an older cousin. Being the youngest of the three they would usually gang up on me, and I remember one incident in particular. We went to Sunday School in the local Bethesda Chapel, in our best Sunday clothes; a walk of about two miles. The path led over waste land which had been built on at one time and the buildings later removed. One Sunday we discovered a large hole in the ground filled with soot by some long-gone chimney sweep. The older boys jumped over it quite easily and challenged me to do the same. Being much smaller I landed in the middle and emerged covered in soot, my best clothes ruined; a serious matter indeed.

In the old days people had to pay to see a medical doctor and that could be expensive. Many could not afford it so there was often a sort of "wise woman" who acted as the local midwife and who was called out to the sick. She would also lay out and wash the dead.

My grandmother's sister, called Aunt Emma, was one of these wise women. She had had an accident with a tram which left her somewhat lame and with a club foot. She was a little strange and she had a psychic gift about which I remember hearing as a small child. Renie Rowley, one of our family, was brought up with her and was endowed with similar gifts. When in later years she had become a Christian, we ministered together at a healing service in Buxton, Derbyshire.

On my father's side also there seemed to have been a healing gift – amongst his aunts – and one in particular was well known for it. Maybe something was passed down from that far distant relative.

Surprisingly too the Chapel had a Healing Ministry, and Pastor Jeffries used to attract large crowds for healing.

During my years at Longton High School, Stoke-on-Trent, when I would be about eleven or twelve years of age, I became friendly with a boy who was the organist at Shelton Parish Church. It was through him that I began to attend that friendly "middle of the road" church and came to be confirmed.

Just before I was due to receive the laying on of hands I became ill with scarlet fever and was confined to my bedroom for some weeks. When I finally went to be confirmed I remembered seeing a radiant light for the first time which bounced, like a little ball, all the way from the sanctuary down the church and into the nave. Many years later I would see this same dancing blob of golden light bouncing round my bed when I was serving in Sierra Leone, West Africa. Maybe my confirmation contained in it the first hint of the body of light which was to play a large part in my mystical development in later life.

During my teenage years I lived in a world of books. While still at the high school I helped out at a library, changing books. This opened the whole of the library to me. I was particularly fond of a young lady assistant, and I was broken-hearted when she left. I spoke to my mother about it and she told me ". . . these things happen and we have to accept them, but remember that once we have become attached to someone we always remain in their heart." I found that very comforting and have since passed on these wise words many times.

It was during this period that I began to be aware of my own psychic ability. I remember there being nobody in my immediate family who could explain it to me and I found it difficult to talk about.

I remember going to the cinema one Friday evening – another world of make-believe – and my hands became very hot and painful. My Aunt said that maybe my hands should be used in the Lord's service in ministering to other people. That was the closest I got to an explanation.

Instead I found myself turning to Jesus, the unseen companion, and talking to Him, and also listening to Him in the privacy of the bedroom. It was a two-way conversation.

It was not until late in my teens that I realized this was not a common practice, indeed that it was somewhat unusual, and I became rather frightened. Fortunately I met a woman on holiday who was able to talk through these gifts with me and to reassure me that there was nothing to be afraid of.

When I was about seventeen we went to Wallasey, near Liverpool, for holidays and to stay with two sisters at a village just outside the town. One day I was on the pier by myself and could not believe my eyes when I caught sight of one of the sisters at what looked like a palmist's booth.

This was unthinkable to me, that such a fine

21

person should be so engaged in what appeared to me to be a tawdry, unworthy occupation. I was very upset and did not know what to do. Later I blurted out my feelings to her and she told me that she made her living telling fortunes.

Despite this, it was she who helped me to come to terms with my psychic gifts, and prophesied that I would go to South Africa and marry five times! She did not get the correct part of the continent; I did go to Africa but it was to Sierra Leone, where, as I shall describe, my idea of God became more fully shaped. Of the five marriages there is still no sign.

The Vicar of the Parish of Shelton was the Revd Guy Parkhouse, and I was fortunate to become friendly with him. His wife had died just before I met him. They had no children so I think in a way he adopted me as one of his own.

We became very close and would go on long walks together in the countryside round about Mowcop, Staffordshire. Although he was between seventy and eighty at that time he was still able to walk for miles.

I had considered entering the Church and sought his advice. He had not done so until his middle thirties and advised me that the best thing to do was to have a job first and then see how my vocation would work out. Consequently I became a student of the University of Birmingham in 1950/53, where I took an Honours degree in History. I was all set to take a second degree in Sociology at the London School of Economics when my Appointments Officer suggested that I should try for the Colonial Service, since I had specialized in West African history as part of my degree.

I took his advice and was granted an interview which proved to be successful.

Chapter Three

SIERRA LEONE

In those days the Colonial Office appointed by telegram. Unfortunately when it arrived at my home, offering me a post in Sierra Leone, I was in Yugoslavia. As a student job I used to work for the United Nations and had taken a party to Yugoslavia in 1953 just after the end of the Second World War. My parents were frantically trying to locate me. When I eventually returned they said that I had been appointed to Sierra Leone and none of them knew where that was. It was known as "the white man's grave" due to its unhealthy climate. Some of my relatives frightened my mother by telling her that "they all die of drink over there". So not only was she afraid of my dying there, she was also afraid of my dying drunk. Certainly on my first trip out to Sierra Leone by boat I did notice that a familiar breakfast for most of the old colonials was brandy. I had never before seen people drinking so early in the day.

Six of us, raw recruits, arrived to take up our positions as Assistant District Commissioners.

My first impression, as the ship was landing, was the particular smell of Africa, which I will probably never lose. I was to stay for thirteen years.

When we arrived we were all destitute, having been students at the London School of Economics. The first thing we did was to go to the bank to get credit. Money was a big problem in the early days, because, although we were only Assistants, we were expected to maintain the standards of living of "the raj". We had to have a first and second cook, a first and second steward, and a gardener. On our abysmally low pay we could barely afford to keep ourselves. We had to dress for dinner, all of us, whatever the circumstances. We were obliged to buy these expensive togs and also elaborate cases and trunks.

A very senior officer in Freetown, one Derek Hughes, arranged for us to appoint servants, etc. When we went to Government House to witness the signing of the Government House Book we were told grisly stories about previous recruits. One had never been forgiven because he went to greet the Governor with a cigarette in his mouth.

We were asked about our schools and our background. Most of the recruits came from a similar background, and either their parents or grandparents were known, or they themselves knew serving officers.

In those days "the jewel in the crown" was of course India and, after India, Malaysia. The least exalted was Africa and, in particular, Sierra Leone. Gold Coast and Nigeria were tolerable but Sierra Leone came well down at the bottom of the list.

The colonial civil servants did a good job in their own fashion. They were honest and hard working. Many of them, however, had no time for the Africans. The women in some cases actively disliked them. It amazed me that they spent so many years in these foreign countries yet despised and disliked the people in whose lands they lived.

Once we had seen a bit of Freetown life; had been to the club, which is the great British invention; had employed our servants; and got some cash from the bank, we each set off for our first station.

Whilst I had been in London, at the LSE School of Oriental and African Studies, I had learned a native language called Mendi, and had struggled and sweated over it. Naturally my first posting was to an area of the country where they spoke a completely different language, Timni, so I had to begin all over again.

I boarded a train for a place called Makeni. The journey took sixteen hours and we had very little food. I was accompanied by my first steward, a very likeable rascal called Joseph. He had been in many European households and knew all the tricks, but he was not bad for a start.

We arrived in the dark in this strange place and were met by my first District Commissioner, Philip Birkenshaw. I stayed with him for the first day since there were no hotels in these provinces. You stayed with whoever would put you up, usually the DC or an engineer or someone of that rank. At our first meal we wore evening dress and mosquito boots. I saw the insects for the first time and one of them landed in my mulligatawny soup. Afterwards I was taken to my own house, a temporary building with a tin roof and a minimum of Public Works Department furniture. There was no bath, no bathroom and no running water.

My first meeting with the Commissioner of Northern Province did not get off to a good start. He always said that I did not like him, and maybe that was true. He was not very pleased when I insisted on having a bath installed in my house and went myself to Freetown in a lorry to collect it.

In my first station I was very ill with malaria, a weakening illness with high temperatures, vomiting and an inability to eat. The German doctor and his wife were very good and nursed me through recurrent bouts. Even now when I have a cold, all these years later, I still get this fever and chill, a residue of my time in Makeni.

Makeni was very lonely indeed, until I got used to the people. The District Commissioner's place was also a temporary building, with a thatched roof and a marble lion sitting outside his office. The Commissioner, however, had a modern building with air conditioning – a great luxury. I little thought that in a few years' time I would be occupying that office.

We had no refrigerators and so had to live mainly on rice and meat. I had no car, and used to stagger up the hill from the office with the temperature at 100 degrees or so, and the Commissioner or the District Commissioner would drive past, never thinking to offer a lift.

The few Europeans in Makeni would meet at the weekend for dinner parties. Some people drank quite heavily. Saturday lunch would start about one o'clock with drinks, and these would continue until about four o'clock, by which time I would be feeling desperately hungry. I soon discovered that the answer was to eat before going to dinner parties.

I was befriended by the local Police Chief, whose mother was quite well known as a writer of romantic novels. He used to take me up to their house most nights, when he would drink quite heavily and fall out with his wife. I also remember the wife of the District Commissioner, newly married, coming out. She looked absolutely beautiful in a light dress and a big floppy hat.

We learned our job by sitting in on the work that the DC did in his office, interviewing complainants and going on trek. I was in Makeni for about nine months before being transferred to my second station, a place called Magburka. There I had a much more modern house, a bungalow type, but I still had quite a distance to travel from my quarters to the office, usually without transport. I attended a training college which also was a long way away. I made some friends there and got to know the local people in a much deeper way. And I began to go on trek on my own without the DC.

The tribal chieftains all provided a rest house for the use of visiting officials. This would be a wattle building kept in a fairly clean condition. One chieftain in particular, a very respected "ohadji", used to decorate the walls of the rest house with colourful hand-woven country cloths. Unfortunately I had to give a judgement against him and he was not very pleased about it. I wondered whether the drapes would be missing the next time I visited him, and sure enough they were gone.

I began to learn about the secret societies, the "Porro" – the Men's Society. This was a kind of government within a government, and a lot of decisions were taken by them. The Chief who was in charge as far as the Europeans were concerned, may well not have been the real leader of the Porro. Once we trekked far into the bush to visit a chieftain. Shortly after I returned riots broke out, and the Chief and the other important men who had been entertaining me had to flee from their own people.

We had a special sort of police force of our own, called "court messengers", who acted as orderlies and escorts and, when we went on trek, as guards. With the aid of our "court messenger system" we were supposed to be the eyes and ears of the DC but we were caught unawares by these riots. They were a movement of the ordinary people against the paramount chiefs and others in authority. I visited a place called Matotoka and found myself surrounded by thousands of Porro warriors. They wanted to burn the rest house, with me and the paramount chief in it because I would not agree to his removal.

Back at Magburka a very hostile situation quickly developed and we had little protection except our own courage. However, my friend the Police Chief mounted a rescue. He was not afraid to claim casualties, and was awarded a gallantry medal.

After nine months of Magburka it was time to go on my first leave, having served for eighteen months. Before I could get away I was visited by none other than the Chief Commissioner himself.

I told him that I hoped I would not be moved to Freetown on my return – and that of course was exactly what happened. However, in Freetown it was at least possible to get an overview of developments in the whole of the country, instead of being confined to a particular district.

At this time Independence was looming, and Europeans were preparing to hand over to Africans. Possibly the riots helped to speed up the final declaration in 1961. A new Governor, Maurice Dorman, was sent out to arrange the transfer of power to the people of Sierra Leone. The Europeans felt that it was not yet time for this and some did not like Dorman, but he came from Stafford and I came from Stoke-on-Trent so there was a sort of instant bond between us.

One day the secretary called to say that I was to be moved from the Ministry of Works to a desk at Government House. I protested and the secretary got annoyed because this was supposed to be some sort of honour. In the end I found myself working in the Secretariat in the daytime plus Government House part-time. This meant that often I would work from early morning to the early hours of the next morning. Eventually I was appointed aide-de-camp to the new Governor, and moved into the special flat in Government House. There were deadly boring dinner parties, night after night. My strategy was to start off by having a large gin and tonic and to keep topping it up with more tonic.

People were rated according to a system. Those at the bottom of the pile could be invited to pre-lunch drinks. The next category could be invited to pre-dinner drinks. Then came those who could be invited to lunch, and at the very top of the pile were the ones who could be invited to dinner. This last category could include a mixture of Europeans and Africans, which was a great development at that time.

I remember, in the early days in Makeni, the Commissioner of the Northern Province asking me whether it would be suitable for a young officer to have a meal with all of us. He was the protégé of his Bangura and had been trained at Sandhurst, but despite this, at that time it was unheard of for an African to have a meal with Europeans.

One night, before I moved into the flat in Government House, I went for a meal with my great friend, Tom Skuse, who was the Director of Surveys and Lands. An interesting person, he did a lot of broadcasting and was an "uncle" in the radio *Children's Hour*. He remained for quite a few years after Independence and was one of my last friends to leave. After that dinner it was quite late when I returned home, only to find that all my clothes had been stolen. All that was left was a dinner jacket. Having little money I had to borrow what I could and somehow keep up appearances as aide-de-camp to the Governor.

Even in normal circumstances being aide-de-camp was a demanding job, and you had to be certain you got things right. If he was going to attend a function I had to map out the place, check out the time it took to do the journey, and also check on the people he would be meeting, and so on. Protocol demanded that when the Governor arrived and stepped out of the car the National Anthem would strike up immediately. If it did not, or if there was some other hitch, I would be certain to receive a telephone call asking me to report to him. Lady Dorman was even stricter, but on the whole we got on very well.

We admired the Governor for the way he threw himself into the job. He was full of life, full of energy. He enjoyed meeting the people and helping the colony to prepare for Independence. If he was not popular with some it may have been because they had been appointed with many years of career prospects, only to find in 1961 that they would soon have no job at all.

There was a "blacklist" compiled by the new Sierra Leonean Prime Minister and the other Ministers. Many of the senior Europeans were on it. All they could do was to take their compensation and go. Some were glad because they had been used to controlling everything themselves and found the new situation difficult.

The Governor was not very sympathetic regarding the difficulties of these Europeans. Some years later he shared their fate when the Prime Minister announced in Parliament that the Governor, now Governor General, was leaving the country. He was very upset because he had not been consulted.

In 1954 the Governor of Sierra Leona sent for me and said that he wanted to make me Acting Provincial Commissioner. I was twenty-nine, and would be the youngest man to hold that rank in the history of Sierra Leone. When he asked if I thought I could do the job I replied, with the supreme confidence of youth, that of course I could.

The job entailed running an area the size of Cheshire with six District Commissioners, all of whom would shortly be Sierra Leoneans with the coming of Independence, each running his own smaller area. It would have been impossible to achieve that position at my age before the era of Independence, but most of the senior white Europeans had left the country. I was to enjoy several happy years, moving from province to province, before the country was taken over by a military coup. Had this not happened, I suppose I should have remained until the present day.

The province for which I took responsibility was Bo. Working with an African Minister was not always a bed of roses because of the old antagonism between African and European. Fortunately many Africans really loved me. They said that, although I was white, I had a "black heart". Certainly I had an unusual rapport with them.

As Provincial Commissioner I now travelled extensively. It was my task to train Africans to take over the posts of District Commissioner. Many Ministers wished that they had been able to keep or indeed to recruit new European officers. The problem was that the Africans belonged to their own tribes and had their own family loyalties. It was difficult for them to be detached and impartial.

The ruling political party came mainly from the south and were for the Mendi tribe, who had been educated by foreign missionaries. They had enjoyed power for twenty years but opposition had been steadily growing, particularly in the more Muslim north. Resisting both coercion and bribery, I had to report to the Prime Minister that the whole of the Northern Province, where I was then the Provincial Commissioner, was unreliable.

The first Prime Minister had been a doctor, Dr Margai. He had been married to a European in his youth. He was a highly respected man and, looking back, an astute politician. He kept the reins of government firmly in his hands until he fell ill and died.

He was succeeded by his brother, Albert Margai, under whom the party lost power. The Europeans had always said that Albert would be a disaster as Prime Minister. He certainly had no love for Europeans, saying that their smell always affronted him. I was by this time the only European in the administrative service, and was brought into contact with the Prime Minister through my good friend Madam Ella Coblo Guilama, who was the first woman Minister in the West Coast of Africa. Some said that she was his girlfriend, but certainly it was Ella who kept my career going in the Sierra Leone of those times.

I met the new Prime Minister on a regular basis and was friendly with most of the Ministers, many of whom I had known as young clerks many years previously. Those in power thought that it would be the best thing for the country, and certainly for the Party, if it became a one-party state. I travelled round the country with the Prime Minister in my own areas while he tried to persuade the chiefs and people to accept the one-party system, driving amongst thousands of people, sitting beside him in his white Mercedes Benz, and everywhere the dancing and merry-making went on.

The approach of 1967 brought trouble for me. My reports showed that there was little chance of the Party winning in the Northern Province in the forthcoming election, but they did not believe this. I came under suspicion of being a European offering unwelcome advice.

The election results were inconclusive. The Prime Minister was arrested by senior army officers whilst having drinks in the army mess. Quite soon the other Ministers, many of them my personal friends, were taken to the local prison in Pademba Road, Freetown.

As I was sitting drinking my sundowner, I heard the local radio announce that the army had taken over the government and that Provincial Commissioner Fisher should report immediately to Freetown. I knew it would be unsafe for me to travel to Freetown as ordered, and delayed going for about two weeks, but effectively my job as Provincial Commissioner was over. Fortunately, as I said earlier, I had known most of the people now in authority as young men, so I was merely transferred to the tourist department in the Secretariat, where I suppose they thought I could do least harm.

I remained there for a few months, then applied for leave, left my position, left my possessions, came home and never returned. I knew what it was to be a refugee. If they had known that I was never going to go back I might have had trouble going at all. My chief steward, Bobo, took a job with the Elder Dempster Lines as a steward. After I had left Sierra Leone I was very surprised to learn by telephone that Bobo was in Liverpool and hoped to come and see me. Our meeting was my last contact with that country, and I have heard little about Sierra Leone since then except what I have read in the Press. I know that the country has been close to bankruptcy. Much of the industry has collapsed. The wealth from diamond mining still continues to trickle away, and the civil war in Liberia has spilled over into Sierra Leone, increasing their financial difficulties. The happy and prosperous days that we enjoyed in those colonial times have sadly long gone.

The most recent uprising was reported in May 1992 under the new military leader, twenty-seven-year-old Captain Valentine Strasser of the also "new" National Provisional Ruling Council (NPRC). The ousted military President, Joseph Momoh, fled the country by helicopter. He recently negotiated a much needed financial "package" with the International Monetary Fund, but whether it will now be ratified remains to be seen.

*

Why have I dwelt upon my time in Sierra Leone? It is only now, looking back, that I can see how much I learned about God there. To the Sierra Leonean, God was as much a part of his life as wife, or mother, or brother. He knew that he was totally in the hands of God. Nothing happened in his life that God did not know about and was concerned about. For the African, God is not some being "out there" – far away, remote; God is someone who takes an active part in their lives. Maybe this was because of the poverty and the awareness of death that was always with them. God was one of their few possessions in a cruel and uncertain world. God was REALITY.

Unlike much of their lives, religion was a happy affair. Sometimes we would be in church at Sunday worship for hours at a time. It was in Sierra Leone that I first met the Holy Rollers of the United Reformed Church. It was a grand sight to see the African Christians truly enjoying themselves, freed in the Spirit to dance and roll on the ground in their love of God. It was perhaps a bit too much for me, sweating profusely in my European suit, through hour after hour of "worship" but it was a happy, infectious kind of faith, very simple but very appealing, with an enthusiasm for God not usually found in the ordinary Anglican church.

At the other end of the Christian scale it was the "white Fathers", with their dedication to their building programmes and education schemes, who most impressed me. Like me they really lived and shared in the joys and sorrows and the poverty of the Sierra Leoneans, some of whom thought that I too acted like the "Fathers". Maybe this thought was to affect my own thinking when I returned, looking for employment, to England.

Certainly I was friendly with the Africans and saw no distinction of race or status. One of my senior political officers was quite upset because I talked to the office orderlies and asked about their families. He did not think that this was fitting at all, and said that I would never make it in the Colonial Service since I was acting more like a social worker than a political officer. Living as I did for most of my service "in the bush" it was natural that my daily life was spent sharing in the lives of the local people. I did not have much to do with other Europeans, except for the missionaries, who were mainly Americans.

The African attitude to death was particularly striking. Death was a common occurrence but it was not hurriedly pushed away, as is common in Britain. The deceased continued to be thought of as part of the living family and also a link which connected them to their ancestors. Nobody would take a drink of whisky or any other liquor before they had sprinkled a few drops on the doorstep for "the Old Ones". This did not seem odd to me.

Having complete faith in the Church Triumphant, in the Church Militant and in the Communion of Saints, which are all part of the beliefs of the Anglo-Catholic wing of the Church of England, I had no difficulty in accepting the nearness of the so-called dead, or that we could hear from them from time to time and that we could send out love and prayer to them.

African funerals were group affairs with no one afraid of shouting or screaming or showing emotion as they laid their loved ones to rest. By contrast I was shocked to find, on my return to England, that families would walk away from the grave, either as individuals, not looking at or speaking to each other, or as small groups, without giving one another comfort.

Chapter Four

VOICES

My new job was as District Commissioner in National Savings. I joined the Home Civil Service, bought a cottage in the country, and thought that my life was set on its new course.

My family were hoping that at long last, after roaming around for almost twenty years, I would settle down. I had a job, not dissimilar to the one in Africa, travelling an area in Cheshire, organizing local committees and meeting the general public with the object of selling National Savings. I was happy in my new job and in my new home, especially working in the garden and having extra improvements made to the house.

All this was put in jeopardy by an advertisement I read in the *Church Times*.

The Community of the Resurrection, Mirfield in Yorkshire, had advertised a weekend retreat for working laymen. I had never been on a retreat but somehow felt compelled to apply, and my application was accepted.

Due to work I was late in arriving, and found to my dismay that my fellow retreatants had entered the Great Silence, which meant strictly no talking. I followed the others around for the various addresses and for my meals, and eventually found my way about.

I discovered the chapel below the main community church which is used by the students at the college for their daily services, and was sitting quietly in this small church when I heard a voice saying out loud "I want you for a priest".

I looked round about me because I had thought I was alone. Maybe I had overheard a member of the Community talking to a student. To my surprise there was nobody there.

As I have mentioned elsewhere, I have heard voices all my life, mainly interiorly but also occasionally exteriorly. I had considered the priesthood when I was seventeen or eighteen. So far as I know I had no intention at that time of becoming a priest but, as many others have also discovered, this "call" or whatever it is does not entirely go away.

We could not break silence, and the only way I could talk to anybody was to put my name down for an interview with the Retreat Conductor. That was what I decided to do, but when the time came I funked it. I was not able to tell a complete stranger, monk though he was, that I had heard the voice of God talking to me. I babbled something inconsequential and escaped.

I decided to confide in my local parish priest who was also a friend and who had served in Africa. He listened quietly as I told him my story. He said that the Church had a special body called the ACCM who tested vocations, and he thought that the best thing I could do was to write to the church authorities – in this case the Bishop of Chester. He made the wry comment that though the Church was not God, it might be able to give me my direction.

With great misgivings I followed his advice and wrote to the Bishop, who recommended me to sit for a Selection Conference. I went to Whirlow Grange in Sheffield along with other candidates. One was an ex-Navy type who seemed to be more on my wavelength than the other seemingly "pious" candidates, and we got on very well indeed. We used to enjoy a little "nip" together after all the prayers and interviews.

I must confess that I did not expect to be accepted by the ACCM, as most of the other candidates seemed to be highly involved with their local churches and much more used to worship than I was. The most I had had to do in church services in Africa was to read the occasional lesson as senior political officer in that station. I did not think I had done well against such opposition.

To my horror the Church Selection Board seemed to agree with my "voice" and recommended me to go forward for training for the priesthood. I was most upset. I had just bought the cottage of my dreams, had a good job and did not relish the thought of starting yet again from the bottom. There seemed to be no alternative. So ended my second career.

I remember telling my mother what I was doing. She said, "You are completely crazy, you are always doing crazy things", and we had quite a row about it. Neither my mother nor my father were church-goers, although my mother had sent us boys to Sunday School. Throughout her long life her view of church-goers was never very high, especially of those who were much involved in church work. She could not understand the gossiping and back-biting. Her attitude to my latest change of career was probably understandable.

I had spoken to her about Confirmation for several years, but she was not confirmed until she was sixty-seven, when the Vicar of the Crooked Spire, St Mary's and All Saints, Chesterfield coaxed her to go through with the ceremony. I think she basically remained a Methodist up to the end. She had a very personal faith and trust in the Lord Jesus Christ. When she was very ill and close to death I asked her if she had said her prayers that night and she

45

said, "Of course I have. Trust in the Lord."

When I came to look for somewhere to train for the ministry, it seemed appropriate for me to return to the "scene of the crime" as it were, and I applied to Mirfield Theological College. I chose Mirfield also because of the prayerful surroundings of the community of monks; Matins and Mass; Mid-day Office; Evensong and Compline.

This Community of the Resurrection, as it is called, has been going now for over a hundred years, and was formed by a group of men who felt moved to meet together for prayer and worship and to provide means for the training of priests who were too poor to be able to afford the education. Thus they hoped to bring Christ to the slum-dwellers of their day. They set up a hostel in Leeds where men received the necessary training. Perhaps their most respected figure of recent times is Archbishop Trevor Huddleston.

There are various compartments in the Community. There are the Friends, who are their general supporters, and there are the Oblates, who have their seat in the choir but are not on a par with the resident monks.

There was a separation between the College and the Community. The Brethren were not encouraged to know the students at that time, but we could use the upper church for some of the Masses and for our meditations after breakfast, before lectures started. I also tried to have a period of meditation after tea – about 4 pm each day.

I have always felt that the prayer support at Mirfield was of particular help in the Ministry of Healing and especially for work in a parish. It is sad that the offering of the daily Mass is no longer such a part of the Church of England witness. Many churches are locked except for Sunday worship, and the clergy do not say their Offices.

I may have entered Mirfield partly on account of the surrounding of prayer, but I little knew that the course of studies laid on for "elderly students" entailed writing an interminable number of essays. Several times I wanted to rebel and to chuck it all up but, through the friendship of another "elderly" student, I persevered. He found writing essays easier than I did because he had been used to doing reports and was able to extract the essentials out of several books and to put the gleanings into some sort of order.

It was unusual for a student to be admitted as an oblate but Eric Simmonds, who was later to become the Superior, that is the Abbot of Mirfield, persuaded the Principal of the College, William Wheeldon, to let me do so and I took out simple vows of poverty, chastity and obedience. Although I felt called to the religious life it was considered necessary to have experienced parish life first. By the time I had completed my service in my first parish of Styvechal, Coventry, the novitiate had already been closed and remained so for some years so I could not join the Community at that time. I have remained as an oblate ever since and I have been grateful for the prayers and assistance of the Director of Oblates, Father Gabriel Sandford. He has been a true friend.

I always felt part of the Community and regularly visited Mirfield later in life expecting, I suppose, at some stage to become a full-time member. I wrongly assumed that this was inevitable.

However, by the time my mother died in 1990 and I was free to join, the Brethren felt that I was too old, nearly sixty, to be able to follow the Rule in its entirety.

Having "passed out" from College I had to get fixed up with a "title" or parish. I was really committed to the Diocese of Chester which had sponsored me for training. I looked at several parishes and remember hastily rejecting one where the vicar told me that he was very keen on the Healing Ministry. He has since become very well known in that field, but I remember thinking that none of that cranky business was for me! I was still looking when I met again with a friend from College who had become a vicar in the Coventry diocese. I asked him if he knew of any "decent places" and he recommended two. I only looked at one and got fixed up on the spot with the Rev. Harry Puntis, who had also been trained at Mirfield. I remained with him some years both in Styvechal in Coventry and the Crooked Spire, the Church of St Mary's and All Saints in Chesterfield.

As soon as I had agreed to go to work in the Parish of Styvechal, Coventry a letter arrived from the Bishop, who was unknown to me. He said that if I was thinking of coming to his diocese it was perhaps better that we met. This was my first encounter with Bishop Cuthbert Bardsley.

My relationship with Bishop Bardsley has probably spoiled me for all other bishops. He had the gift of making you feel that you were the most important person in the world, the subject of his undivided attention. Whenever I visited him to administer healing (for he was one of my first patients) he always came to the door to meet me with a smile. After our meetings were over he would escort me out. It was also Bishop Bardsley who brought the Fisher Folk to England and thus introduced the modern hymns now so familiar in *Mission Praise*.

Bishop Bardsley solved my first problem: that the Bishop of Chester was determined that I should serve in his diocese. He wrote to the Bishop of Chester; I was let off the hook and went off to Styvechal to train as a deacon.

Father Harry Puntis, the Vicar of Styvechal, was known in the Diocese of Coventry for his role in the training of deacons. At that time he had three or four other curates, some beginning as deacons and some looking forward to moving on to a senior curacy. He and I never had a cross word in the whole of the four or five years I was with him. He was a dedicated priest and what I learned from him greatly helped me in other parishes, starting with my first one which was at Chesterfield.

As deacons in the Coventry diocese we were expected to submit a series of essays to the tutor appointed to look after us. This involved a good deal of reading. One of the subjects I started to read about was the Healing Ministry in the Church. One morning my tutor told me that he wanted me to meet a Mrs Rogers who was a well-known healer. He thought that this could help with my thesis. She was visiting the diocese to minister to the Bishop and also to lead a Healing Service which was being held in Coventry Cathedral.

My first reaction was to refuse. I did not really want to meet any cranks and certainly not some weird healer so soon after being ordained and starting my new career as a deacon. After being at the top of the tree in my first career in the Colonial Service I was finding difficulty in adjusting to being back in my own country. I just wanted to serve my title in the ordinary way without becoming involved with a new hierarchy in the Church and to concentrate on working out my new identity. However, being used to obeying orders I decided that I had better do what the tutor suggested and reluctantly went to see Mrs Rogers.

When I asked for her at the new cathedral I was told that I would find her in one of the underground chapels of the old bombed-out cathedral ruins, where she was at prayer. I went down the steps into the chapel, and after I had been sitting quietly for some time a grandmotherly figure came over and, much to my surprise, placed her hands on my stomach.

She was a large, powerful-looking lady with blond hair; well dressed and with a face radiating kindness. I thought that my worst suspicions had proved to be correct. All sorts of doubts and fears flitted through my head. Then I began to feel a warm glow entering my stomach and a fire seemed to be coming from her hands. Some of my patients have likened this feeling of warmth in the body, distinctive to the Ministry of Healing, to having a hot water bottle placed on them. After a while she told me that at times I got over-tired and sometimes rather muddled in my mind. This was true. I had not found it easy to become a student again, and greatly missed Africa and the life I had known there.

She then introduced me to a clergyman whom she said helped her in her work and who would be able to help me with my tiredness and my muddled thinking. He took me to the altar, laid his hands on my head and began what I now know to be an exorcism. His hands began to shake violently and I felt as though my head was being wrenched off my shoulders. It was quite painful. I remember thinking that being with cranks was turning out just as I had feared, and that a headless deacon would probably solve the problem for itself.

He said later that an African witch doctor had come over with me. This did not sound as preposterous to me as it might have done to most people. In my work as District Commissioner in Sierra Leone I had naturally come across the secret societies which existed there. During my treks into the interior I had had many society members dancing for me. In my work as magistrate I had, without doubt, crossed some of the leaders, especially during the riots in the colony in 1955/56. Perhaps the witch doctor's presence, if it were true, accounted for my nostalgia for Africa and my state of mind which I had put down to too much change in the months since I had left Sierra Leone. At any rate the exorcist declared, at the end of his ceremony, that the witch doctor had departed and I had been freed from him. By this time I had developed one of my headaches and was feeling more tired than ever, in fact quite limp. I later discovered that my new friend was a well-known exorcist in the Church of England with a parish in Hampstead.

That was my first experience of the Ministry of Exorcism, in the crypt under Coventry Cathedral. It is a ministry I have avoided. I was once asked to minister to one of the vicar's patients on her way from Birmingham to see him in London. At that time I was seeing patients in an upstairs room in my house in Styvechal. I was suddenly aware of a great sense of evil, hastily said a prayer, threw some holy water around the room, and ushered the lady out of my house, fearing that this spirit of evil would be left behind after she had gone.

The second experience was when I was ministering with Mary Rogers and laying hands on one of her patients. Suddenly such a foul smell rushed from the patient's mouth that we were both appalled. Again we got rid of the lady as quickly as we decently could.

Though I believe there is a need for the Ministry of Exorcism, and that it has a valid role in the ministry of the Church, it is not one in which I would wish to be involved. I feel it is a dangerous ministry and can lead to great difficulties for both the minister and for those ministered to. In the diocese there is usually one clergyman who is known as the Diocesan Exorcist, with special permission from the Bishop.

My encounter with the exorcist was not the last surprise of that day, for there was another surprise to come. Mrs Rogers said that she thought that I, myself, was a healer and would be able to help her with the sick people who would be coming to the cathedral in the afternoon.

I had known for many years that I had a psychic awareness but, as an adult, I had always tried to keep that door firmly shut. It had, however, greatly helped in my work in Africa. On this occasion I thought I should help in return for what Mrs Rogers had done for me. I must also confess that I was curious to see what would happen during the ensuing service at the cathedral.

When the people lined up for healing, Mrs Rogers took my hands and guided them to various parts of the sick person's body, explaining what was happening. I remember most vividly one woman, who had come with a hearing problem, cry out at the heat from my hands when I put them over her ears. Also my hands began to vibrate, all to my great astonishment. It seemed that I had intuitively located the area of pain and begun the healing work myself.

At the end of that first healing session I remember I felt so dirty that all I wanted to do was to throw off my clothes and jump into a bath. This was a combination of panic, shock and conviction of unworthiness. Who was I to bring healing to people? Events were moving too quickly. I had merely set out to write a paper and here I was, caught up in something I did not understand.

Later I accompanied Mrs Rogers when she visited the Bishop in his office, to give him healing. She told me he was suffering from a bleeding ulcer. The Bishop said how much better he had felt since receiving healing. He had had an interest in the Healing Ministry for many years and had been a close friend of Dorothy Kerin, a pioneer healer, who had finally established a Healing Home at Burrswood and done some really outstanding work for the Church in this particular field.

To my astonishment Mrs Rogers said that in her absence I should continue to heal the Bishop and that he had agreed to this arrangement. Thus ended my plan to serve my time as a deacon as quietly as possible and to stay out of the limelight.

Mary Rogers, an inspiration to me in the early days, deserves a book all to herself.

The wife of a Labour MP, George Rogers, living in Harrow, she knew most of the members of the Cabinet in Harold Wilson's time. It was said that she even came into contact with the Royal Family and other great houses. She also knew many of the current stars of screen and radio, including sporting personalities, some of whom I met when I visited her. Most of her Healing Ministry work was done on a one-to-one basis. She worked very hard, seeing people throughout the day and into the early evening, followed by answering correspondence.

She had been a member of the United Reformed Church, but was baptized into the Church of England by the Bishop in his own chapel, with only the three of us present. However, I understand that, in later years, as Mary was dying from cancer, she was admitted into the Roman Catholic Church. Her mother had been a staunch member of that Church and they especially had helped Mary, during our tour of Australia.

Mary had a great devotion to the saints, especially St Francis and St Agnes. This belief in the Communion of Saints was another bond between us. When later we toured Australia we felt that Padre Pio and St Martin de Porres were particularly helpful to us in our ministry.

It is difficult for some parts of the Christian Church to understand the difference between Spiritualism and the Communion of Saints. In Buxton I had great difficulties due to my involvement with Padre Pio and Alice Jones. I understand that at least one parishioner wrote to the Bishop saying that I was a Spiritualist.

There is nothing like that involved in our work. It is a matter of recognizing that the spiritual world also impinges on this material world, and that Jesus Christ with all the saints is the bridge between them and us. He has been given full power and authority by God the Father so there seems no point in dealing with deceased human beings such as doctors when we can have the full healing power of Christ flowing through us. So, while I am committed to the Ministry of Healing I would not wish to heal by the practices of the spiritualists.

Like me, Mary lived in a world of her own. This is what happens to a healer. One feels, as it were, that one has one foot in Heaven and one on Earth. Because of our need to be aware of the spiritual world, we seem to live a life apart from everyday concerns.

That is not to say that Mary was a saint. She could have a fearsome temper at times, although, in all the years we knew each other, we never had a row. She liked life and was extravagant. If she was given £100 in her hand she would quite likely buy a new outfit or take someone out for an expensive meal.

I found myself going regularly to the Bishop's house for his healing sessions in 1971 and 1972. I remember going to heal him one morning, travelling along in my car. The lights showed red, and as I was waiting for them to change I heard an interior voice saying to me "Heal his back". When the Bishop greeted me I said to him, "Bishop, this morning I have not to heal your ulcer; I have to heal your back." To my amazement he said, "Well, that's very funny, Eric; I have just been to Coventry Football Club for physiotherapy and indeed it is my back that needs healing."

The Bishop's problems responded well to the healing and he never failed to express his gratitude in writing. I have kept his letters and they were a great encouragement to me, coming as they did at the beginning of my ministry of healing. Here are extracts from two of them:

Monday 10th.

Just a line to thank you very much for the wonderful healing that God gave me through you. Despite great pressure of work I have been much fitter and the pain has nearly gone. If you could come once more that should complete the cure. Could you possibly come at 10 am on Friday?

December 18th.

I want to thank you very warmly indeed for your great kindness to me. Thanks to your ministry I am feeling wonderfully better. Alleluia. Perhaps if I have further pain I may come to you in the New Year. I thank you for your ministry with affection and gratitude.

It was the Bishop who sent me to my first individual patient, a lady suffering from inoperable cancer. When I met Queenie I saw that, although getting on into middle years, she looked as though she was pregnant. I did not know what to do. So I said to her, "I've been sent by the Bishop to pray with you, so that's what we'd better do." I laid hands on her and said that I would come again the following week.

As the weeks progressed the cancer of the ovary, from which she was suffering, gradually reduced in size. To her delight she was able to wear ordinary clothes instead of a kind of smock, and was able to go to a wedding a year later and to dress up. She became a regular member of the church, having lapsed for a considerable time, and took part in our ladies' choir.

One day as I went to do the healing I found her vacuuming the carpet and I thought to myself, "That's it. It's going to start all over again." Not long after that her husband phoned to say that Queenie had been taken into hospital, and so I went to be with her. I visited her until she died, to pray with her and to put on a bit of scent because she was always very proud of her appearance.

When Queenie died it was about Christmas time. I had caught her earlier pushing the heavy vacuum cleaner and told her that when Our Lord called her He would say, "Come along Queenie, I have just the job for you. Take a duster and polish the stars."

In the Christmas post I received an envelope

and inside was a picture of Queenie dusting the stars. She had asked an artist friend to draw it. You can imagine my shock on opening that envelope. I have kept that picture all these years. I suppose our first patient is the one we remember best of all.

In Coventry I first discovered what I can only describe as the gift of diagnosis. Mary Rogers had said to me, "You can put away your books. God will show you the pictures and diagrams He wants you to see just like an X-ray." I thought that was rather strange at the time but have since found similar views expressed by J. Cameron Peddie (of whom more later), who says in his book that it is God, the Holy Spirit, who is the one and only complete and unerring diagnostician and healer. We leave both the diagnosing and the healing entirely in his hands. (*The Forgotten Talent*, Ch. 5), so we do not need to worry about it.

One example particularly impressed me in those early days in Coventry. A man came to visit and told me that he had been diagnosed as having cirrhosis of the liver. Immediately up popped my own diagnosis, "No, it is not cirrhosis of the liver, it is hepatitis." When the man went away I looked up these diseases in order to learn something of their nature. A few weeks later the man telephoned to say that he had been to the specialist, who said that he had been mistaken in his diagnosis: what he was suffering from was not cirrhosis but hepatitis.

This has happened many times through the years. Somehow an interior voice is able to give me something of value about the patient's ailment. These diagnoses have often been confirmed by the doctors and surgeons. I remember in Coventry a patient was admitted to hospital suffering from a cancer form of leukaemia. Prior to admission he used to visit me before attending the specialist, and I was able to give him, in advance, his blood count and the white blood cells, and so on. The specialist took great delight in checking out my diagnosis when he was doing his tests. We had quite a game between us until the man eventually died of his disease, having lived longer and in greater comfort due to the combined efforts of medicine and healing.

During my time in Coventry I used to meet with Mary Rogers in London for her advice on healing, and quite often I would help with her own patients. It was during one of these trips to Mary that another key event took place.

I was with her when an Italian lady arrived. She used to call on Mary when she came from Italy on visits. I noticed that she was very disturbed, so I excused myself and left the room. When I returned some time later the lady said to me, "It's not *you* I did not want to have in the room. I hate all priests. There is only one I like and that is

Padre Pio." That was the very first time in my life that I had heard about Padre Pio. So it was that I came to read and to learn about him.

My vicar, Harry Puntis, was eventually appointed to a post in Chesterfield, but I remained in Coventry for a little while until the new man took over. Then on a visit to Mary Rogers I suggested that the next time she went to Australia I would go with her, and she agreed. This visit turned out to be six weeks of intensive preparation for the Healing Ministry, and I have described it in greater detail in chapter seven.

It was 1978. On my return I had no job to go to, so I wrote to Harry, who urged me to join him in Chesterfield. He had been interested in the Healing Ministry for many years. He did not feel that he himself had the gift of healing but, like Bishop Bardsley, had taken an interest in the work of Dorothy Kerin and the Home of Healing at Burswood. So we began to conduct a series of healing meetings. He had great skill in conducting such meetings; offering a prayer at an appropriate time. His prayers were absolutely wonderful. He was an inspiration to me during this period and I continued to learn more every day. The Healing Ministry has a fascination difficult to describe, perhaps because we are given glimpses of the Holy Spirit at work in the lives of ordinary people.

At Chesterfield I acted as chaplain to the Royal

Hospital. Some years previously, when I had been discussing the Healing Ministry with my Principal at Mirfield Theological College, he had said, "The best way for you to learn and to get to know about this healing business is to become a chaplain." I remembered this advice and one day, when I went to a gathering of clergy, the Bishop of Derby invited me to go to the parish of Buxton. My first answer was "no" but he asked me again, and this time said that he wanted me to go as the healing member of the team. In 1978 I left Coventry, and one of my roles in my new post was being chaplain to the three hospitals there. It proved to be an opportunity to gain further knowledge of medicine and the practical side of healing.

It was during this period that Stephen, a young boy of about seventeen who worked in a butcher's shop, was healed. It was an important staging post for me in the learning process.

Stephen was admitted to the Cancer Hospital with cancer of the testicles. His mother was told that it was very serious indeed. A parishioner of mine asked if I would see her, and although they were not church people I thought I might be able to help them. I went to meet them and began the healing.

Stephen hated hospital. It took all his mother's powers of persuasion, and mine, to get him to go. I would visit at home, after his medication, when he was vomiting badly at night. I would pray with him, the vomiting would clear, he would go to bed and next morning he would be back at work in the shop. At the hospital Stephen was given treatment which might have killed an older person, but he was able on each occasion to take up his job in the butcher's shop immediately afterwards.

Whenever I was laying hands on Stephen I had the most foul taste in my own mouth. The only way to get rid of it was to suck boiled sweets. This was what he was tasting: the result of his chemotherapy, and I tasted it too.

At the end of his medication and treatment his woman doctor told his mother that she should go back to Buxton and say she had witnessed a miracle.

At first every week after his discharge from hospital Stephen came for healing, usually on a Sunday morning. This was later extended to monthly sessions until he felt that he no longer needed the treatment, but, during the years I was at Buxton, he would call on me from time to time.

My first encounter with chemotherapy was worth it in Stephen's case, because he is thriving up to this time, 1992, and working full-time in the butcher's shop.

Another outstanding case in 1970 also concerned a young man. I was asked to visit a boy called John who had had his back broken as a result of a rugby accident up in the North. The boy had been taken into a hospital in Sheffield well known for its work in spinal injuries. His mother, Winifred, was the wife of a doctor, and I believe that her faith greatly helped to pull that boy through.

I used to visit every week. It would take three hours, one hour there, one hour at the hospital and one hour back. When I first met John he was unable to move his head. He was unable to move his arms or his legs and they had said he would never walk again. Gradually as I prayed and anointed him he began to improve, until the day I remember particularly, when he was released from the hospital. He stood by the car and for the first time I knew that eventually he would be able to walk.

We continued with the healing; his mother brought him all the way from Windermere down to Buxton where we had the healing sessions. I am glad to say that John did eventually walk. I was delighted to take part in his wedding and am also able to report that he now has two children of his own. Looking back it was wonderful to see John, whom we were told would never walk again, walking, albeit in a somewhat spasmodic way down the aisle for his wedding.

Winifred has continued to keep in contact with me all these years and usually telephones me when prayers are needed for John, or when he has to go for further tests in hospital. As an illustration of the ongoing nature of this case, Winifred told me recently that John is to have surgery to remove a cyst from his spine. Apparently this is a complicated operation and we will be praying as before, this time for the success of the operation. Often the Healing Ministry is seen as a single act, whereas in many cases numerous services are required, sometimes stretching over years.

I am not sure how the healing has affected his own faith. Being a young man he found the Healing Ministry difficult to accept in a hospital ward of men. No doubt he was teased by the others, eager for some good-natured banter to relieve the tedium, and quizzed by the curious, but the treatment continued. John knows that his mother is in regular contact with me, and he has had his two children baptized, from which we conclude that his faith is real although he is not demonstrative about it. No one is forced into the Kingdom by the Healing Ministry. The door is always left ajar and some walk away. Others need time to assimilate the significance of this tremendous thing which has come into their lives.

John's sister has been much involved in show jumping, and their mother telephones me when she is taking part in a trial. She is now qualifying for events such as Badminton and mixing with all the great names in this sport. Winifred and I usually pray together for her safety when she is doing a cross-country competition. This apparently is a particularly dangerous part of the trials.

I have not had much contact with John's father, the doctor, but he has become Church Warden in his church and is active in the life of the village. I believe he is very highly thought of, both as a Christian and as a doctor.

About this time, 1984, I was coming to the end of my contract with the team ministry in Buxton and was looking around for somewhere to go. For some time I had been helping with courses for the clergy in Sheffield, training them in the Healing Ministry. I had a wonderful dinner given to me by the Bishop of Sheffield, and it seemed to be just a question of finding a parish to go to in the Sheffield diocese. In the meantime the Bishop of Derby asked what I was going to do; what did I want to do? I said, "What I really need is to have a parish as a base, with a small congregation; a place where I will be able to concentrate on the Healing Ministry." I had been doing the job of hospital chaplain, looking after two churches and running my own healing work, so I felt that I needed to lessen the strain for a little while. So the Bishop of Derby very kindly gave me the parish of Shirland, and I was to stay there for four and a half years.

From Shirland I began to travel about the country. I also made visits to Rome and Germany and began my work in Portugal. For three years I went to Portugal every two or three months for the Healing Ministry; again a most wonderful time, learning healing on the job. These sort of things have stood out in my life, but I never failed to be grateful for the majority of the blessings of the Holy Spirit which, though less spectacular, have been high points in the spiritual lives of the people concerned.

In 1989, I was again to be approached by the Bishop of Sheffield. He had heard on the grapevine that I might be interested in the parish of St Matthew's, Sheffield. During my visit to Sheffield, when I had been training the clergy in the Healing Ministry, I had called in at the lovely church of St Matthew's, which was really the Anglo-Catholic Shrine of Sheffield.

I decided to have a closer look and I liked what I saw. I met the people concerned with the appointment. We agreed and forthwith informed the Bishop. So I became the Vicar of St Matthew's, Sheffield.

In addition I was appointed to be the Bishop's adviser on healing, but so good had been our training that many of the parishes were already engaged in healing. There was little for me to do in that regard except to act as a kind of resource for the diocese.

It was during my time in Sheffield that Scottish Television came to make the now famous film on Alice Jones and her healing involving Padre Pio. It has led to a further extension of the healing work. For example, I was invited to hold two missions in Ireland and one in Scotland, all of which were richly blessed, in addition to my normal day-to-day ministry.

This then was my apprenticeship for the Healing Ministry. It has been interesting to see how many apparently unconnected occurrences have led me, little by little, to my present position. It is not a life I would have chosen when I first set out, but it has been rewarding in many ways. Those who choose to travel with Jesus may at times be terrified or acutely embarrassed or frustrated, but seldom is the journey dull or boring.

I have found, like my mentors J. Cameron Peddie and Mary Rogers, that as time goes on the number of patients increases, the requests for prayer multiply, the healing service grows and the whole of one's life pattern alters.

Healing becomes a way of life, spreading throughout the day, and then into the evening, until bedtime. It demands dedication, consecration, sacrifice, sweat, tears and a good deal of personal pain. It does give tremendous rewards, in the love and care of people of all sorts and conditions, and a growing nearness to God. It satisfies many needs in our own lives but in the end it may be easily summed up. Healers heal because they can do no other.

Chapter Five

HEALING IN PUBLIC

People are naturally curious when they hear that there is to be a Healing Service in their neighbourhood. What goes on at these gatherings? Is it just an ordinary service with some rather dubious prayers for sick people? Or is it the work of some extreme sect from the fanatical fringe, best avoided?

Usually you will find that it is a service during which people in need of physical, mental or spiritual healing go to the altar rail to receive a blessing or unction, which is anointing with oil by a priest. There may be hymns, periods of prayer and sometimes a short address or explanation. If there has been a previous healing as a result of one of these services, the person concerned may tell their story.

Nothing very remarkable you might think? You would be wrong.

Look at the people around you. Some you will recognize but there will be others you have never seen before. Some may have travelled long distances in the hope of getting some relief from their pain or their problems. This is not an ordinary Sunday morning congregation.

No one will ask why they have come or what their form of religion might be, if any. They are simply treated as individuals who have come to us in need. All who are sincere, and not merely curious, will receive something, great or little. I know this because the healing power does not proceed from me, the healer, but from the Lord Jesus Christ through the power of the Holy Spirit, and we can be sure of Him.

When I begin to heal it is as if I am stepping into a column of pure white light which extends about a foot in front of my body. When I stretch forth my hand to lay it on someone's forehead it is His hand that is placed there. Small wonder that many collapse, "slain in the Spirit" as it is called, and helpers have to be ready to catch the person and to lower them gently to the floor, where they recover after a few minutes, usually much elated.

I knew that it was important to communicate the real source of healing power to the participants in the Healing Service; but how was this to be done? Fortunately there was an answer to hand.

From early life many Christians have identified the person of Jesus in the Blessed Sacrament. So by carrying in the Sacrament, the consecrated bread from the Eucharist, which is reserved or kept in the Lady Chapel, and laying it on the High Altar, in full view of everyone, we demonstrate His presence amongst us and so we are reminded that His is the power acting in our midst. The exposition of the Blessed Sacrament on the altar emphasizes the centrality of Jesus. At first I thought it might be difficult for people of other Christian traditions to accept this, but somehow the whole service comes together through the hymns, the Bible reading, the explanations and the testimonies. Members of the congregation are invited to go forward for anointing, if they wish, and the laying on of hands followed by the Benediction.

This form of service has an atmosphere of its own which surely confirms that Jesus is truly present with us according to His promise, "Lo, I am with you always, to the end of time." Indeed I know this to be so because each time I raise up the Sacrament I see the face of Jesus. It is not always the same. Sometimes it is His young face; at other times it is older and burdened with care, but always it is a great joy to me to see it; almost too great a joy at times.

A well-wisher once described our Healing Services in Chesterfield as a mixture of doctor's surgery, confessional and interview without much, if any, mention of God, Jesus or the Holy Spirit. In spite of countless services in my various parishes of Chesterfield, Buxton,

Shirland, Styvechal and Coventry I still doubt whether we have got the "mix", if that is what it can be termed, absolutely right. This is because people come with a variety of expectations. Perhaps, in view of the many different Christian traditions and set ideas of what is the right or wrong way of doing things, we can never have a Healing Service which escapes all criticisms.

Incredible as it may seem, of all the aspects of the Church's work nothing seems to stir up so much strife as the Healing Ministry. It creates a great love but it can also create hatred and opposition. We need only to look at Jesus' own ministry. It is recorded in the gospels that He did not work many miracles in the village in which he was brought up, such was the attitude of the people, who refused point blank to believe that there could possibly be anything remarkable about this local boy. "Why, he's only the son of that poor couple, Joseph and Mary, and we know all about them. He might be able to bluff others but not us."

As a result of this opposition, for a time I stopped holding Healing Services altogether although I continued to work in private. However, when I moved to a new parish in Derbyshire, the parish of Shirland, I felt that it was time to begin a public Healing Ministry once more.

When Alice was healed and able to walk once again, some in her church rejoiced but others said, "It's just a confidence trick. Once Father Fisher has gone away you will be unable to walk again." It takes faith to hold on to a cure or healing when this happens.

If the necessary faith is in such short supply it should not be surprising that in any parish only a relatively small number of people support Healing Services by their active help and by their prayers. Maybe such services are more likely to attract the non-church-goer, and the lapsed or irregular members of congregations. They are able to come into this atmosphere without feeling out of place in a congregation. Also those who are more timid or nervous can more easily come into church for this special ministry.

Many attending feel a real need either for bodily healing or for healing of the soul. Some, like the widow in the gospels, have tried everything else to no avail and there is no other place for them to go. In my experience it is often such people who may well receive instant healing.

For instance, at one service a woman came to the altar where she told me that she had just come to please her husband adding, "I don't really believe in all this sort of thing". I smiled and asked what the trouble was. "My back", she replied. What she did not tell me at that time was that she spent her afternoons lying in bed because of the pain. Indeed she doubted if she would be able to sit through the service. I laid my hands on her back and she returned to her place. Her back was healed instantly.

Later she presented herself for Confirmation, became a full member of the Church and she is still a practising member nearly twenty years later.

In Coventry healing usually took place during the Service of Holy Communion, after the Confession and Absolution and before the person received the Sacrament. It was there that I met another healer, a Mrs Ingram. She used to visit Styvechal about once a quarter for the Healing Services.

After one Service Mrs Ingram showed me her hands. They were covered with a slight film of oil, quite apparent and distinctive. In his book *The Forgotten Talent* the Rev. J. Cameron Peddie suggested that this is the oil referred to in St James' letter (James 5:13–15). He writes (page 85):

I always took it for granted that the oil referred to in healing was some form of man-made oil such as olive oil. I never would have dreamed of thinking otherwise but the Lord had something else to tell me on this question and he told me in a most convincing manner.

It happened when I was giving a service to a brother minister and my hands were on his brow and face. Suddenly he said to me, "Peddie, your hands are oily. You are anointing me with oil." I lifted my hands and we both looked at them. All over them there was a film of oil with solitary globules here and there. It was no illusion; it was a physical reality. In a little while he said, "Peddie, the oil is perfumed," and so it was. It had a strange sweet pleasant aroma.

Of late I too have noticed that my hands are more oily when I am healing than when I am not.

Mrs Ingram continued to help the clergy at Styvechal for many years. The Vicar of Styvechal was later appointed to Chesterfield where, after a Healing Mission to Australia, I joined him. An excellent feature of the services in Coventry and Chesterfield was that lay people would assist the clergy in the healing, both lay and clergy taking part together.

One lady called Avis continues to help me to the present day. She first came to me when her husband was diagnosed as having terminal liver cancer. She fell on her knees and pleaded, "Please help my darling Jim." I said, "I can't help you but I am sure that the Lord will help him through our prayers."

Jim was a wonderful recipient. The healing would flow through him and he would fall into a deep sleep. Instead of only living a short time, as was expected by the doctors,

Jim lived for a further three and a half years.

Avis began to help me and we discovered she had a special gift. She has continued to help people all over the country, and often takes part in Healing Seminars in the South of England.

The gospels record that Jesus sent out His disciples, two by two, to heal the sick. I think I understand why they went out in pairs. It is a fact of human nature that we both attract and repel one another. Given a choice of two or three healers, the patients will choose one or other for their trust and faith. For example, a man who was desperately ill with cancer received healing from Avis in the Lady Chapel, Chesterfield. He made a wonderful recovery which lasted for a considerable time. He was able to drive hundreds of miles and took his wife and family away on holiday. When Avis was not available he would come to me but later, as the end drew near, he would ask for Avis.

People came to Healing Services in Chesterfield with many different physical and spiritual needs. They came from a wide and varied cross-section of the Christian Church – Methodists, Baptists, Roman Catholics, Pentecostalists and Anglicans, all united to minister and to receive in the name of Jesus Christ.

Often ministers or priests would come with their own groups and, if spotted, would be asked to take part in the service in whatever capacity they wished. Others would prefer to remain in the congregation quietly enjoying the service, but later some of them would come forward to take on the work.

Experiences like this show that Healing Services can provide a bridge for ecumenical activity. We are all united by being baptized in the Lord Jesus Christ. In Chesterfield the services usually began about 7.30 pm and lasted for about two hours with a short break about nine o'clock to enable people who had to leave early to do so quietly. Chesterfield Parish Church, I must confess, was a very cold place indeed. The chill would seep up through the stone floor and people would freeze, but still they came.

At St Matthew's in Sheffield the Healing Services last about an hour and a half, but as the numbers increase the length of the service will inevitably increase. A copy of the form of service is reproduced in Appendix Two, as a guide to anyone wishing to organize such meetings. Naturally it would have to be changed to suit the traditions of the people involved. St Matthew's is a church in what is called a Catholic or Tractarian tradition in the Church of England. The ceremony may not be familiar to everyone but our helpers are always glad to explain it. Although it may seem strange at first, it does seem to work and to bring us all together in the presence of the healing power of our Lord Jesus Christ.

I am very conscious of the time factor. It is

difficult for people to sit still and quiet for long periods. I try to take the children first; then any wheelchair cases, and lastly the regular attenders. People keep coming up for healing, and they need to. Instant cures are relatively few. It is the systematic laying on of hands which helps most people.

Often I know in advance, through letters or telephone calls, about those who are critically ill, and I spend more time with them. In addition I engage the healing members of the team to minister with the more seriously ill patients.

In Chesterfield the first part of the service usually took the form of a short introduction to the theme of the evening, to welcome the people. This theme might, for example, be based on the Holy Spirit's gift of love, joy and peace. Then there would be a reading applicable to the theme, followed by a short explanatory talk. Then came open intercession when another member of the team would lead the congregation in prayer. Next the names of those in need would be called out, and these people would be lifted up to God in prayer. Some of those later reported how they had felt upheld, peaceful and warm after their names had been called out aloud.

People who received healing were encouraged to give witness. It was noted that a special kind of silence was experienced while these people gave their testimony. Other people felt this testimony was helpful in strengthening their own faith.

The laying on of hands usually followed after the intercession. In Chesterfield some people required the Blessing and others required personal ministry from the healers. For the Blessing a prayer was said along these lines: "May the power of God Almighty, Father, Son and Holy Spirit flow through you, restoring you in body, mind and spirit." It was not always easy to differentiate between those who were in need of the Blessing and those requiring the laying on of hands; some sought both.

After the concluding prayer and blessing the congregation were invited for a cup of tea. This provided an opportunity for anyone who wished to discuss their problems more personally with the team.

During my stay in Chesterfield several people expressed an interest in becoming healers, and I used to invite them to help at the Healing Services. This provided an experience difficult to acquire in the Church of England. Having additional help enabled the queue to progress more smoothly.

Healers have to learn patience and understanding. Each person comes with their own special need. One friend, who lives alone and has suffered a stroke, told me that he had never been touched with such a feeling of tenderness and

ABOVE A picture of me during my time in Sierra Leone (*Chapter Three*).

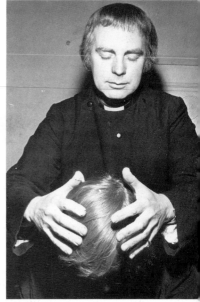

RIGHT Healing a Coventry newspaper reporter in 1972.

BW

The **BISHOP'S HOUSE, COVENTRY**

CV5 6PW

Telephone Coventry 72244

13th June, 1975.

My dear Eric,

       Naturally I was sad to read that you are leaving the Diocese after your Tour in Australia, but I am delighted to know that you are going to continue your work with Mary and that you will be concentrating on the Church's Ministry of Healing in Chesterfield. This is good news indeed and I pray that God will richly bless your ministry there.

       Of course we must meet before you go, so please get in touch with me again nearer to the date of your departure.

       Yours ever,

THE REVEREND ERIC FISHER

THIS PAGE AND OPPOSITE A selection of letters from the Bishop of Coventry, Cuthbert Bardsley, thanking me for healing him.

The **BISHOP'S HOUSE, COVENTRY**

CV5 6PW

Telephone Coventry 72244

Monday 10th

My dear Eric,

Just a line to thank you _very_ much for the wonderful healing that God gave me through you. Despite great pressure of work I have been much fitter - the pain has nearly gone. If you could come once more, that should complete the cure.

Could you possibly come at 10.0 on Friday? If not, perhaps you cd. fix an alternative time with Betty. With deep gratitude, however,

C.C.

Tuesday

Alternative.

I can never be sufficiently grateful for your great kindness to me, & to also thank God that He has endowed you with such gifts. To pray that - if it is right - Bromwood may be willing to have you, & that God will richly bless your ministry there -

God bless you,

C.C.

LEFT My early inspiration came from Mary Rogers. This picture used to adorn her letterhead.

BELOW The picture of 'Queenie dusting the stars' (*pp 61-2*). She was my first individual patient other than the Bishop.

Christmas ✳
Blessings.

ABOVE LEFT Padre Pio has inspired and guided me since my early days in the Healing Ministry. (*See pp 63-4*.)

ABOVE RIGHT The late Revd J. Cameron Peddie, author of *The Forgotten Talent* – an inspiration to me and to many others in the Healing Ministry. (*See Appendix One*.)

BELOW Annie Parissot, who gave me relics of Padre Pio.

LEFT The picture of Marius Franck, showing the diagram I drew to aid me in praying for the healing of his brain tumour. The joyful result led to my first individual Healing Mission abroad – to Rome in the following year, 1986. (*See pp 99-102.*)

RIGHT Vivian developed leukaemia at the age of thirteen, but recovered after receiving healing. He was healed a second time later in his life when he badly injured his head. Doctors were amazed when he survived and his brain was found to normal.

My next mission was to
Portugal. These two pictures
were taken during Healing
Services there.

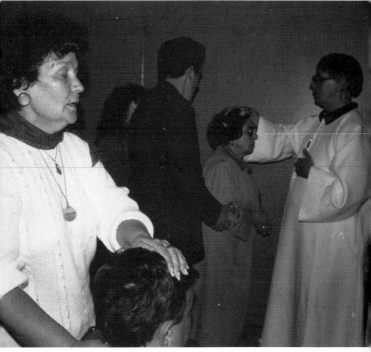

ABOVE LEFT Sarah's brain tumour was arrested through healing. She died in 1991, several years later.

ABOVE RIGHT Isobel Henderson with 'Chloe'. Her sight improved through a combination of medicine and ministry. (*See pp 91-5.*)

BELOW Alice Jones in church at Haydock in 1991. *The Guardian* featured her story in a piece about the case for Padre Pio's canonization. (*Guardian/Denis Thorpe*)

sympathy as when he received healing. In Chesterfield, under the guidance of Father Harry Puntis, we were fortunate in experiencing an atmosphere conducive to the healing process. A conscious effort was made to avoid an emotional atmosphere. Father Puntis had a great feeling for the conduct of a meeting. Sometimes we did, however, notice that he was moved by the Spirit; even dancing a little in that Spirit.

What should your attitude be when you attend a Healing Service? I think that we should be calmly expectant and we should hope always for a miracle. But the Lord does not guarantee instant cures.

God works, God is active and God moves in His world. The solution you receive may not at first be the one you hoped for. In fact, you may simply need as a first step the spiritual strength to live with whatever you are suffering from. Even this is a big step forward. Faith is the essence of healing and needs to grow in each one of us. Your initial session might be the first of many as your faith is strengthened and your problems recede. By whatever means, some are healed, many are relieved and all are comforted.

Chapter Six

HEALING BY
TELEPHONE

The telephone procedure and others like it are so
simple that a gentle warning may be in order.

It is easy for the helpers to fall into the trap of
thinking that it is they personally who are
providing healing, when in fact they are only
channels for God's healing grace. The "healer"
is generously connected into God's great powerhouse of love and so makes the necessary energy
(or call it what you will) available, even at a
distance, to be passed on through the hands of
the helpers. Some would say that such a one had
been given a gift of healing. Peddie would say
that it is not strictly speaking a gift but rather a
capacity which, under God, can be developed.
Another warning: do not think that because
your ministrations were "successful" yesterday
all you have to do is to repeat the same
procedure in every detail for the same success to
happen today. That would be verging on magic,
which has no place in the Healing Ministry.

Instead we have to listen to what the Lord is saying to us and also we have to listen carefully to the patient. Out of this listening we can learn what we should do. This is one of the necessary gifts of the healer: to be a good listener.

Much can be learned by examining the findings of other healers, such as the Rev. J. Cameron Peddie. In his view the healing powers are imparted by the Holy Spirit but are controlled by Jesus to match the need and receptive powers of the patient. He supports this by his own experience in the laying on of hands. The volume of power is modified in various ways, gradually increasing in strength and, when enough has been ministered, gradually decreasing. This accords with my own experience.

The team, consisting of the healer and (usually) two or more local helpers, provide the faith which needs to be present for healing to take place and also there is often the support of various prayer and meditation groups, known and unknown, who will be praying for the recovery of the patient.

Notice that the patient does not have to have faith for healing to occur but ideally they should at least be open-minded. Many find faith through being healed and we must remember that there is no power in faith itself, only in God's response to it. Likewise there is no power in prayer itself except to make it possible for

God to answer us; Peddie's analogy of the radio where prayer is likened to "carrier waves" over which God powerfully sends back responding words of His love and grace.

If it all seems too good to be true we should remind ourselves that God, whose Spirit can heal us, is the same God who created us in the first place. In doing so He implanted in each of us the capacity for self-healing. If we cut a finger, in time the cut will heal with no help from us apart from keeping it clean. If we are laid low by disease the body's defence resources come forth and tackle the invaders without our intervention. Is it so remarkable that we should be able to transmit these energies to another person in need of extra resources, particularly if we have the approval of our Maker and Inventor to do so? We may never know the mechanism at work but this is also true of the high technology equipment now available to the doctors. Few of us have the remotest idea of how a CAT scanner works, or even the humble X-ray machine, but we believe the results they produce absolutely.

The gospels tell us that Jesus could cure at a distance from the patient and He still can, as we will see in the next few pages.

ABSENT HEALING BY TELEPHONE

Most of the people who are referred to me I never actually see in person. Some write to me and are treated. Some telephone me and I speak to them. Some come long distances for the laying on of hands and prayer, and some attend "telephone groups" in their own locality.

There are now several telephone groups run by local helpers: one in Glasgow, one in Southend, one in Chesterfield, one in Derby and one in Norfolk. The methods are very simple. People who require healing approach the group and a meeting is arranged, to be attended by perhaps three or four people. Any more is very tiring to the helpers, who are seldom young. Sometimes a meeting will be set up for a single person if necessary.

Contact is made by telephone at a previously arranged time when the helpers will give me a brief account of the symptoms and any other relevant information. In addition, as mentioned earlier, I will also exercise my capacity for diagnosis, locating areas of stress or pain in the body or mind of the patient, even at a distance. Sometimes important aspects are left out inadvertently in the briefing which are picked up in this way. For instance, one of the groups introduced a lady recently who was suffering terrible headaches. She also had pain in her cheek which I sensed in my own cheek, though we were hundreds of miles apart, but no one had mentioned this. It was news also to the helpers but, sure enough, the patient confirmed that she had this pain in her face which was causing her considerable discomfort.

In Glasgow, the actual laying on of hands is done by three local helpers, two women and a man for choice, and they are usually lay people. I tell them where to place the hands and the length of time of the treatment, usually ten, fifteen, twenty or thirty minutes. Other people may "tune in" at a distance at the pre-arranged time, meditating on a suitable sentence if they are familiar with the methods taught by the Fellowship of Meditation, or simply praying in whatever manner is most meaningful to them. Others attending the meeting should do likewise without the laying on of hands: three being sufficient.

The patient is seated comfortably and the healing begins with the words "May the power of the Lord Jesus Christ flow through your body, mind and spirit." This is repeated by the three in turn at, say, five minute intervals. The team should be careful of their own comfort. As far as possible they should avoid cramped positions which would distract them from their purpose. Even fifteen minutes is a long time to sustain an uncomfortable position.

While the healing proceeds I will be praying as

I am led by the Holy Spirit. Often the hidden cause of physical suffering is of psychological origin. This could arise from many sources such as loneliness, domestic stress or conflict in the work place. One notable advantage of the Healing Ministry is that the whole person is being treated, not just the symptoms. Benefits can appear which are not those currently being prayed for.

When the patient has been treated for the prescribed time the helpers telephone me again and report what has happened, how the patient reacted, what they felt in their hands – heat, pain or other sensations. The latest tool of the doctors, still under development, is something called microwave thermography. This works by locating hot spots in the body which might indicate a damaged joint or other problem identifiable by the heat generated locally. A person with the healing gift can do much the same through his or her hands as a matter of routine, and thus the hands are guided to the areas where healing is needed.

Finally arrangements are made for the next treatment, usually three sessions being necessary. This simple procedure is proving to be effective, and the helpers are learning more and more of this ministry at each encounter.

It is still possible to apply a variation in this method even if the patient is in hospital. An example of this is going on at the present time. A delightful lady approaching her seventies was admitted to hospital with a coronary, having a long history of heart trouble. I happened to be visiting her part of Scotland at the time and went to see her with the two local helpers. We held an impromptu healing session, simply praying and holding hands, for the ward was very full and very busy. Two days later she suffered a cardiac arrest but fortunately the resuscitation team were able to restore the heartbeat. At first she was unable to reply to questions and appeared to be semi-conscious. The relatives were informed that she was unlikely to survive the day, but next morning a great improvement was noticed and she was able to tell them that she remembered nothing since the arrest. Later is was discovered that the circulation of her left foot was impaired. An angiogram was done and a blocked artery discovered.

By this time I had returned to Sheffield. It was arranged with the helpers that they would attend the patient at precisely one o'clock. We could not count on having screens or access to the telephone. One helper held the patient gently while the other held her hands, and the presence of the Holy Spirit was felt. The whole visit lasted for a mere fifteen minutes or so.

Several days later, a plastic graft was done to replace the artery, under spinal anaesthetic.

Everybody was surprised at how well she stood up to this, but her troubles were not yet over. A few days later an arrhythmia occurred which gave cause for alarm until it was corrected by means of an externally applied pace-maker. This has now been disconnected and she expects to go home in a few days. This is a good example of one of the Peddie "Laws" (Ref. 5), which states that the Divine Healing Power enables a patient to derive more benefit from the doctor's treatment than would otherwise be the case.

Another interesting example selected from many cases is also on-going and concerns my friend, Isobel Henderson. She is well known as the author of three books on Contemplative Meditation and many papers on the subject, which she has personally presented at gatherings of the Fellowship of Meditation up and down the country. She is one of the longest serving members of the Fellowship and was a friend of the founder, Marion Dunlop.

There are many books on meditation but Isobel's books do not merely discuss the subject. They teach the reader how to do it with a beautiful simplicity. I often use her papers on tape for my daily meditations.

All this writing is the more remarkable for one reason: Isobel is blind and has been from the age of twelve. She relies on her faithful guide dog, Chloe, the fifth in a long line of hounds as remarkable for their intelligence as for their appetite. In a blind person the labour involved in writing a book is immense, quite apart from any research of the subject which may be required.

I had given Isobel healing earlier in the year and indeed had travelled north to continue the treatment. Her health was causing her many friends some concern. Privately, she doubted if she would ever have the strength to write another book. It was quite a few weeks later that she saw "the light" – not a supernatural light, though you might disagree. One night, lying in bed, she became aware of what she later called a "globe" of light. She opened and shut her eyes several times. It was still there. She lay looking at it. Then she remembered. That afternoon she and an engineer friend had been given a demonstration of a Braille computer. He had left his coat in the bedroom and maybe switched on the light to find it on leaving. She jumped out of bed and sure enough the switch was at the "on" position. She stood switching it on and off, seeing something for the first time for over fifty years.

A telephone link-up was arranged with the local helpers and I asked Isobel to keep a diary on tape, which she did with her usual thoroughness. This runs from January 1992 to the time of writing and hopefully beyond. Our objective was of course to have her sight restored, even if it was only to the degree she experienced as a child before its slow decline, year by year.

At first she became aware of light and dark and saw a fuzzy outline of the dog and the glint from the chrome handle of the harness. The following session she described as "very powerful". At lunch she could see the contrast between the plate and the tablecloth. In particular the movement of her hands holding cup and saucer could be seen. Movement could be detected but not quickly enough to steer clear of objects if she was herself in motion. She was seeing what she called "brilliants" — bright sparkles of light, sometimes of a golden colour. This seemed to impede her sight. She struggled to penetrate through this curtain of light particles. She did her best when the "brilliants" were no longer getting in the way.

Disappointingly, the sessions now appeared to be less "successful". She could still see bright things such as the taps and the wash-handbasin when she knew what she was looking at. She was gradually losing ground and objects were becoming more misty and less defined. At the same time she felt conscious of things happening in her left eye in particular, suggesting to her that it was being worked upon. Tongues of light played back and forth across the eye while she was engaged in her morning meditation. She felt that something was going on; preparations of some sort. This went on every day for two weeks.

By this time her sight was on a kind of plateau: a considerable gain over her initial state but not clear enough to be useful in identifying objects.

Then came a new insight. She remembered the Cameron Peddie "Law" (Ref. 6), that where healing is not sustained we should look for a medical or surgical solution. Her eyes had not been checked for over forty years because she had been told, even as a child, that her sight would fade and absolutely nothing could be done about it. At this point there came about one of those happy coincidences which defy statistics. A doctor called on an entirely different commercial errand which required an examination. He advised her, *en passant*, that she should see an eye specialist as he thought she might have a cataract in one eye. This proved to be the case, an operation was carried out, and it was also found that there was glaucoma in both eyes which would have been painful if left untreated. It had already done quite a lot of damage. It would be necessary to get the pressure down to allow stimulation of the nerves and blood vessels which had begun to shrink. Hopefully something could be reclaimed.

To understand what follows we have to appreciate that over the years Isobel had become used to being blind. More importantly, she was convinced that her blindness was being used in her writing. Over the months she began to ask herself if this new quest for sight was in fact a distraction from the work to which she was dedicated. She began to waken in the mornings with the words "unfinished business" ringing in her ears. What if the healing she had received was intended to give her the strength and enlightenment to write another book? She felt sure that she would not be given her sight merely for her pleasure and convenience. If she got more sight it would be because her work was changing. Meanwhile, all this was preventing her from getting down to her work, so, for the time being the sessions have ceased.

Already Isobel is halfway through writing the new book. She has been given the necessary strength and hopes to be given more sight in His good time – after the book is written. She will not be distracted by what she calls "divided loyalties" from this "unfinished business", which is how she sees it.

This is her choice and I respect it.

Chapter Seven

HEALING OVERSEAS

Our tour in Australia was, in a sense, my real apprenticeship in the Healing Ministry. Although I was getting useful experience in Coventry I learned much more by assisting Mrs Rogers in Australia.

Mary was already well known there. If healers have a preferred country, as I found during three years of visiting in Portugal, then Australia was Mary's country. She was treated almost like a queen over there.

At the time of our visit in 1978 Mary had recently come out of hospital after a cancer scare and in fact we had considered cancelling the trip. With healing she was pronounced fit enough to make the journey, which was horrendous. We were almost two days on the flight. I remember Mary sitting with her legs on top of the next seat. Her feet began to swell up. It must have been a painful journey for her, so recently discharged from hospital, but she made no complaint.

When we arrived at the airport in Perth she was immediately besieged by reporters. I was so exhausted that I did not feel I could face them, but there she was, after the hospital and that long journey, full of life, ready to lay hands on the reporters and to say to one, "You have back trouble. Let me heal your back." So began our Healing Mission.

Perth was a most beautiful city, beside the sea, with an almost colonial air about it. At that time there was very little outside the city except for a lot of desert. We were treated very well. I really enjoyed Perth. I lived in the grannie flat of a lady who had come from England with her daughter, Yvonne, and we soon became great friends. You will remember the gospel story about the woman with a haemorrhage. She had spent all her money on doctors but received no cure until she touched the hem of Jesus' cloak. While I was in Perth the daughter, Yvonne, was healed of a similar condition.

During the day we worked in church halls or mission halls, seeing people who had been recommended to Mary on a one-to-one basis. We also had Healing Services which were well attended. Probably the largest single attendance was at St John's Church in Melbourne. We stayed there for about a month, and one night two thousand people crowded into that church. Some travelled for hundreds of miles to be there. It was an electrifying experience ministering to all those people. Some in the crowd were healed without even receiving the actual laying on of hands. In particular two cases occurred in this church which stand out for me.

One evening a nun called me out of the service and asked me to say a prayer in the porch for her friend who was blind and could not get into the crowded church. I laid my hands on her and suddenly she cried out, "I can see!" "What can you see?" the nun asked. "I can see a red coat", was the reply. As the healing continued so the formerly blind lady was able to see more and more of her friend, who continued talking to her quietly. People were laughing and crying all around us. It reminded me exactly of the gospel miracles when the onlookers were amazed.

The other case took place one night at the end of a very long session. A boy came who was born deaf. In all his life he had never heard any sound. He had come for healing before and here he was again. It was about midnight. We were all exhausted but the crowd laid hands on him, whereupon there seemed to be a mighty rush of power and suddenly the boy could hear. A miracle in fact.

Mary Rogers seemed to have great energy. She could continue the healing long after I was tired. She would stand there, laying hands on people and being supported by the helpers.

During this trip an interesting aspect of Mary's character emerged. In spite of all her years in this ministry at certain times she became doubtful of her ability to heal. I have often wondered about that occasional lapse of logic. She was, of course, a very intelligent person and it was as if occasionally her intellect would challenge her faith with the enormity of what she was doing. Who can say? We may never know the way of it.

She enjoyed teasing me in the mornings. I lodged with a community run by nuns quite a distance away. When I turned up she would say, "Eric, you're late! I have had loads of healings already. Several miracles have happened."

My first healing tour on my own resulted from a call from a lady in Rome, in Italy, asking me to help her son, a young man called Marius, who was a teacher in South Africa. He was suffering from a tumour on the brain and terrible head-aches. I asked for a photograph of him.

When the photograph arrived I had a feeling that the tumour was in a certain part of the boy's head. I decided to try to move it out of the head to the side. So as to be as specific as possible I drew, on the photograph, a diagram on top of the boy's head and down the side of the head, and prayed that the tumour be moved out by the power of the Holy Spirit. Afterwards I received this letter, written by his brother:

I think it is time I put something concrete

down on paper in relation to the outstanding events which took place in connection with my brother Marius. The way things developed from the time his illness was diagnosed to the operation and the perfect healing which followed must be made known, in order to prove the efficiency of your prayers and the interest taken in this case during your Healing Service. Most of us at times are reluctant to accept God's Power to the full. Cases like my brother's remove any doubt from one's mind and heart, and just for the record this is how things went.

DIAGNOSIS: Calcification, with tumour and liquid around, which meant it was growing.

This was confirmed by three neurosurgeons in South Africa. This diagnosis, based on elaborate tests, was so definite that the doctor said it was no good having a lumber puncture. Before the operation one of the surgeons said that after the operation Marius would have to undergo radio therapy for thirty days. Before the operation Father Fisher, whom I had contacted from Rome by telephone, told me that something was happening (12th August). In fact up to that time Marius, who had suffered from headaches which had given him terrible pain, for the first time on Wednesday, 14th August woke up without any pain in his head, and that same Wednesday, Father Fisher told me, we are in for a big surprise and that it will be very interesting to see the nature of the thing once they have operated. On Thursday 15th August 1985 he was operated on for about six hours. This was the day of the Virgin Mary's Assumption to Heaven and although being Protestant, both my mother and I had a constant thought the night after the operation of how much Jesus' mother must have suffered for her son.

Anyway the result: the surgeon said he found neither calcification nor tumour. What he had found was a malformation of the veins with haemorrhage which was corrected and resolved by the operation; so Marius is very lucky as he can consider himself a perfectly healthy man.

From the moment he woke from the anaesthetic Marius had no complications whatsoever. The neurologist who filed his case told my mother, "Madam, I will not say anything, just simply that it is all absolutely marvellous; it is the case of the year." Marius, who was aware of what the doctors had diagnosed, was a little reluctant to believe in miracles but his mother, who has great faith, said to him, "You will believe when the doctors will tell you that you need

no radiation treatment after the operation."
The surgeon himself did not know what to
say after the operation and Marius's mother
said, "It was the prayers that did it",
at which the surgeon looked down and
nodded in silence.

It was Marius's sister, Maria, who paid for my
flight to make a Healing Mission to Rome,
which took place the following year in 1986.

I lodged, with a Monsignor Regenie, who was
the parish priest at San Angelo in Rome. He was
a very dear old man indeed. He gave me full
support, not only by making his own church
available for a Padre Pio meeting, but also an
American church where the priest, Father Todd,
at Monsignor Regenie's suggestion kindly offered
me his church for the Healing Services. It had
been arranged before I set out for Rome that I
would also minister in an Anglican church, but
this was not possible since the priest was away.

Monsignor Regenie went in and out of the
Vatican as if he was going home, and I am sure that
it was he who arranged for me to meet the Pope.
One day, completely out of the blue, I received a
letter with the Papal postmark. Naturally I
wondered what on earth it was all about. To my
surprise it was an invitation bearing the number of
a front row seat where, with a crowd of VIPs, I was
to await presentation to the Pope.

When the great day came it suddenly began to rain at 10.30 and the Pope was expected to leave his quarters at eleven. I happened to remark, to no one in particular, "The rain must stop at eleven o'clock", this being a wish or perhaps a prayer. At eleven, as the clock struck, so the rain stopped. My neighbour, an American, turned to me and said, "My God, you must have a telephone link with the high-ups yourself!" and we all laughed.

The Holy Father came down from his "papa-mobile" and began to greet us, so I have a picture of me shaking hands with the Pope which is the envy of all my Roman Catholic brother priests. It was a great honour to meet him face to face. He took both my hands and asked where I was from. Once he knew that I was English he spoke to me in English. I was aware of a great power and holiness eminating from him, and his gaze seemed to penetrate deep into my soul. I cannot remember what he said; I only remember it was a wonderful experience to meet him.

The present Pope is known to be a supporter of Padre Pio. While he was still a humble priest he made confession to Padre Pio in San Giovanni. As Archbishop of Krakow he appealed to Padre Pio for a healing and a Polish doctor was cured of an inoperable cancer. Also, when an archbishop he urged the canonization of Padre Pio, and as Pope has celebrated Mass in San Giovanni, this being one way he can show support for the Padre.

Other Popes have not been so supportive. Some approved and others did not. Pius XII approved. John XXIII, although of similar peasant stock and background, did not. His successor Paul VI was an admirer and relaxed the restrictions which had been placed upon him by previous Popes, such as meeting with people, celebrating Mass and continuing in his work. It is said that the best hope for canonization lies with this present Pope.

In Rome I was also granted an interview with the cardinal who is responsible for assembling the case for the beatification of Padre Pio. In his apartment the decor was predominantly a beautiful scarlet colour – scarlet for a cardinal. As I entered he got up, embraced me and said, "How wonderful it is for you, a brother Anglican, to be pursuing the cause for Padre Pio." We discussed it and he told me that the delay is in San Giovanni. In Rome they were quite ready to proceed.

Since then I have met another cardinal, the Papal Nuncio for Ireland, and talked to him about it. He commented that it is more difficult to get a mystic made a saint than it is for a teacher or some other kind of saint; an interesting side-line on how saints are created. I believe it will happen in my lifetime, although there is said to be a move away from the old-fashioned miracle worker like Padre Pio towards more acceptable saint-like models.

Father Todd's church in Rome was a magnificent building with wonderful frescos, and I have to admit I was a little nervous of how our services would come across in such grand surroundings. I should have known better. As I went to meet Father Todd one afternoon I met a group of African musicians; one of those coincidences which are more than coincidence. They had guitars and were willing to make music for me. Once they knew that I had lived in Africa they were delighted to co-operate. So we began our evening meetings and huge crowds of people came for healing.

My next mission, mentioned earlier, was to Portugal. This came about when a lady called Johanna read about me in the *Journal of Padre Pio*, a publication issued in San Giovanni, and invited me to her country. Not knowing any Portuguese I found this a daunting prospect. However it went ahead. Johanna had been suffering from cancer for some time. She had travelled to the Bristol Clinic in England for treatment. She naturally hoped that the healing extended to others would also be given to her and she was not disappointed. She was the nucleus of my first group. She took part in several Healing Missions and eventually died three years after the first mission. We were great friends and I am sure that she got a lot of comfort and support from the healings offered to her by the group.

On the first mission we ministered in a church. I think that was the one and only church I was able to get in Portugal because the Catholic Church was not really in favour of Healing Services. I was rather disturbed by not having a church to heal in. I wrote to Father Gabriel, who was my Director at Mirfield saying, "I can't get a church. What shall I do?" He replied, "One greater than you didn't have a church and He ministered on the beaches, so why can't you do the same?" That has really been key advice for my ministry ever since. Quite often I have not been able to get a church on these healing tours abroad and have had to minister in rooms or wherever I could. The churches in the various countries are not much in favour of this person coming in to run Healing Services in their territory.

That was the beginning of my close association with Portugal. For three years or so I went every three months to conduct Healing Services, travelling up and down the country, from the extreme north to the extreme south. There were groups of people who gave me their time, their support and their love. These groups did break up eventually and by the end of my time in Portugal I had a much reduced following, but the seed had been sown. Finally I was left in the hands of two people who took me all over the Algarve in their car and we visited towns, villages and tourist centres. At one stage we ministered quite successfully in a holiday camp.

Two evenings stand out in my many memories of visits to Portugal. Once, following a newspaper report, I set out to take a meeting and found the place jam-packed with people, waiting in the pouring rain. It seemed as if the whole population of Lisbon wanted to get in to that particular Healing Service. There were television cameras and crews all around. I was reminded of the crowds who followed Jesus.

I was standing, on my feet, healing from about two o'clock in the afternoon to ten o'clock at night. I cannot imagine people in Britain waiting like that. There was no alternative but to carry on until all were dealt with.

The second occasion concerned a woman who was apparently dead. She was carried into the meeting. They cleared the table, which had a statue and flowers on it, and laid her on it. She seemed quite dead to me and I was uncertain how to begin. I laid my hands on the head and prayed.

The first thing I noticed was a fluttering of the eyes. Then the eyes opened. The hands and arms began to move. After a further period of healing the woman sat up, got off the table and flung herself on me. The whole crowd erupted into clapping, shouting and dancing. It really was a wonderful time and I thought of the words of Jesus, "You will raise the dead if you have the faith."

Angela Bradwell, a Baptist minister, formed a quite remarkable church in Buxton, converting young people who had been on drink or drugs into a group of very able Christians. She had been trained in America where she had gone to Bible college and had developed a real ability for teaching the Bible. Angela and I made three trips to America together during my time in Buxton.

In the 1970s there was a great outpouring of God the Holy Spirit, certainly in America. I felt that God the Spirit was moving in a special way.

The first time I experienced this type of encounter with the Spirit was when I was asked to visit a group of Roman Catholic ladies who had been upset by Charismatic accusations that they worshipped the Virgin Mary. I talked to them and the ladies listened quietly.

At the end of the talk I asked if anyone would like the laying on of hands. A rather large lady said she would, so I asked her to sit in the chair, as was my custom till then, when I heard God the Holy Spirit saying, "Stand her up!" I had quite an argument with the Holy Spirit before I said to the lady, "Would you please stand up?" I laid my hands on her head and the next thing I knew I was falling on top of her on the floor. This was my first experience of anyone, including myself, being "slain in the Spirit" or "resting in the Spirit" as it is sometimes called. By the end of the meeting most of the other ladies had also fallen on the floor.

It occurred to me that this might be a special "one-off" occasion. We were indeed going to a big fellowship dinner that night but, as I rose to pray for the people after the dinner they also began to fall on the floor; a very puzzling situation and I had no idea whether this state of affairs would continue or not. Nowadays we have come to expect it and we have helpers standing by to catch the person and to lay them down gently.

Resting in the Spirit is a phenomenon which causes a great deal of difficulty. The people seem to collapse, to lose consciousness, yet they are aware of all that is going on. In America they simply covered them with a little blue blanket and no one took any more notice of them. I have often asked people who have experienced it how they felt. They invariably say it is a beautiful feeling. They feel relaxed, calm and happy but they don't want to be disturbed. This can be a problem in Healing Services because the space available is soon taken up. In America they got so well organized that people could lie on the floor for maybe half an hour or even longer. I thought that this particular working of the Holy Spirit would be confined to America but it has followed me to Britain and has been part of my ministry ever since.

The action of the Spirit varies with the individual because God meets us on an individual basis. Some laugh, some cry and some are visibly overcome, but all agree that there is nothing harmful in it and it is an experience they would not want to miss.

A strange thing happened in America. I was being driven past a high security prison when I remarked to those present that I was getting a strong feeling that there was bad trouble brewing in this gaol. One of our associates was a guard in the prison and he mentioned it to the chaplain. It was arranged that Angela and I would visit the prison and be shown round. It was a shocking sight to see men chained up like that. We had to pass through lots of doors and I had crosses, etc, with me which kept bleeping the alarm systems.

After visiting the various parts of the prison we were introduced to the Deputy Governor in his office. Straight away he asked me, "How did you know about our trouble?" I told him I had been passing by when God the Holy Spirit told me. He must have found this reply surprising to say the least, but he admitted that there had been a serious incident. Some prisoners had seized a guard as a hostage and were threatening to kill him if their demands were not met. Fortunately the guard escaped and I actually met him amidst great rejoicing.

It is a terrible thing to see human beings confined in that way but even there the Holy Spirit is working. The guards had formed their own group and were praying for both guards and prisoners. Perhaps our unexpected visit showed them that they were not far from God even in that bleak place.

One of the guards knew Angela well. He and his wife had had a horrific accident on a motor bike. They had received wonderful healing, a miracle healing to which they testified in our meetings.

On one of our visits to America we ministered in a huge tent. That trip was quite an adventure. People came from all parts to receive ministry, to play, to sing and to dance in that tent, and clergy from many denominations worked together, including Roman Catholics, Baptists, Methodists and others. It reminded me of the tent of the Covenant in Old Testament times where God was worshipped before the Holy Temple was built at Jerusalem. Later the Roman Catholics distanced themselves from this charismatic healing movement.

Last year for the first time I went on a healing

visit to Ireland. I was invited to go to the shrine at Knock for the Padre Pio day, when thousands of pilgrims who acknowledge Padre Pio gather there. It was a great privilege to go there, to see these pilgrims and to pray with them.

From Knock we made the long journey down to Waterford where we were to hold three meetings in the Butler Community Centre. On the first night, when we went to the Centre, we found it was in a run-down area. Some of the men hanging about looked quite rough. There was a commotion in the entrance and not many people turned up.

On the second night there were more. A young boy called Allan was brought forward, who had had a series of operations. He had not been able to eat any solid food and was fed on a drip. He sat on my knee and we prayed together. When he went home Allan took some solid nourishment, the first for a long time. His mother had been suffering from agoraphobia for years but was able to attend on our last night, and to come forward with Allan, who gave his testimony. People had tried to put her off saying, "It's all rubbish. It's all a great con. Have no part in it", but she had seen what the Lord had done for her child and would not be put off.

Another boy called Keith had had a very rough passage. His mother had not been able to keep him and his grandfather had died of a stroke. As we laid hands on Keith the tears began to flow and continued to flow until the end of the meeting, when he came up and asked, "Why have I been crying?" My helper, Matt, said, "It is because the Lord has given you joy; a little bit of joy in your life."

An unusual witness was a man called Billy. His father had lost both legs and had died some years ago. What had haunted Billy every since then was the thought that they had to bury his dad without legs. He had not gone to church or attended Mass for years. He said that from what he had seen in the Butler Community Centre he felt that once again he could go back to Mass. With tears in his eyes he said to me, "Father, if you had been there maybe my father would have been helped." A bit like the gospels when Martha said to Jesus, "Lord if you had been there . . ." We pray that Billy and his family will now find peace.

On the third night we had a wonderful time together, praising and singing and healing in the power of God, the Holy Spirit.

It has been amazing on these overseas tours how people have come forward to help in many ways, spending time and effort to make the meetings successful. These people have been a means of evangelization. Many have been helped in these meetings and have formed little groups of their own. The leaders come back to me from time to time to report on what is happening in their area.

There is a very active group here in Sheffield which meets on Saturday mornings and which might be seen as a useful model for other groups in the UK or abroad.

I must pay tribute to the support of numerous ladies who made tours possible in their own countries. They include Mary Rogers, Maria Aneda, Johanna and the Baptist minister, Angela Bradwell, who arranged for me to go to America.

The overseas tours have provided great experience in ministering all the day long and doing nothing else. All manner of sickness and disease are brought forward for healing or prayer, each one a witness to the power and loving concern of God, the Holy Spirit. I have seen the Gospel message come alive; where the lame walk, the blind see, the deaf hear and the dead are restored to life. It is my prayer that more of the clergy will come to see this ministry as a high priority in their work and witness.

Chapter Eight

MEDICINE AND HEALING

When I began in the Healing Ministry, twenty years ago, the doctor had long since replaced the Church in the role of healer. In those days most Christian people would never have dreamt of going to their vicar to be healed.

I remember one Sunday night the vicar asked me to go and pray with a parishioner in hospital. The family objected although the man was seriously ill. They thought that if a clergyman went to his bedside the man would fear that he was dying. That was a fairly general attitude and it may still prevail in some quarters. Since that time there has been a growing interest in what has been called alternative medicine. Maybe the interest shown by the Prince of Wales has helped to focus the attention of the public on these practices.

In the early days one of my parishioners came to see me and I felt moved to mention that he might be heading for a stroke. He was a man of violent temper and I was convinced that these sudden rages could have a bad effect on his physical well-being. He visited the doctor and was told, "Go and tell your vicar that physical healing belongs to me; he should confine himself to the healing of souls."

Had this happened today the reaction might have been different. I am glad to say that in recent years I have found a growing co-operation between medicine and the Church. As Bishop Bardsley said on the subject, "For far too long we have left healing in the hands of the doctor, the psychiatrist and the nurse. It is time that the Church took an active part in healing. The Church is concerned to make men holy and to make men whole. Illness can be a form of soul sickness and therefore a concern for the whole Church."

Like J. Cameron Peddie we pray for the time when theological colleges will have Chairs of Divine Healing, and the capacity to exercise this ministry will be a compulsory qualification. A body of respected literature might then result.

How excellent it might be if there were more establishments like Dorothy Kerin's "Home of Healing" at Burrswood, where medicine and the Church work hand in hand together for the recovery of the sick. There is a need to set up many such clinics where doctors, nurses and clergy can work together, dealing with the body, mind and spirit as a unity. There is certainly a growing awareness that health is related to a combination of physical, mental, spiritual and emotional factors, each impinging on the others.

In my own ministry doctors and other specialists have occasionally been prepared to co-operate with me. This gives an added dimension to Healing Services.

Even in the early days I found a difference between the attitude of the local GP and the hospital consultants. As reported in an earlier chapter, a man who had leukaemia came to me regularly for healing, after which he would go straight round to the hospital for treatment. Having usually told him what his blood count was, how the red cells or the white cells were doing, etc, the surgeon would check out my conclusions against his own test results. This continued for about a year until the man finally died in hospital. It was a very interesting co-operation.

More recently I have been dealing with a lady who had Parkinson's Disease and whose body had stiffened up. She was taking a drug which made her almost spastic. I concentrated on dealing with the convulsive movements and, after treatment, she was able to turn over in bed for the first time in years. Previously, if she had wanted to face the other way, she had to get out of bed, walk round and climb into bed again. When she discovered her new mobility she telephoned me in great excitement.

We continued with the healing sessions until one day she told me that she had to go into hospital to have the drug treatment regularized, which could be quite drastic. I suggested that she should inform the hospital. She spoke to the Registrar, explaining that she was having healing and was showing some improvement. The Registrar's reaction was, "Well, we don't know everything. Carry on with the healing!" and admission to hospital has been postponed.

You may ask whether there is a risk to the patients in that by administering healing we may delay or even suspend urgently needed medical treatment. J. Cameron Peddie deals with this in chapter seven of his book, headed very appropriately, "God's Ally the Doctor".

Pain is often a warning that something is amiss. Healing relieves pain so it could be argued that there might be cases where it could be dangerous to apply healing, thereby obliterating the warning. Peddie describes the case of his own son who suffered acute pain in the middle of the night. Peddie prayed and laid his hands on the affected area. The pain abated only to return with equal severity when he removed his hands. This was repeated for half an hour. The pain would vanish when the hands were applied but would return when the hands were removed. By this time he knew that this was a job for a doctor or a surgeon. He rushed the boy to a hospital where acute peritonitis was diagnosed; one of the worse cases the surgeon had dealt with. Indeed the doctors doubted if he would recover sufficiently to work again, but with the combined forces of medicine and healing he was released from hospital ten days later to convalesce in the country.

Peddie concludes from this and other similar cases that, where it would be dangerous to remove pain by the ministry, the pain either refuses to disappear or it returns when the hands are removed from the patient.

Elsewhere he says, "The Holy Spirit is the only complete and unerring diagnostician and we leave the diagnosis and the healing in His hands."

People ask how I know on which part of the body to lay hands. This is a combination of influences. Obviously the patient will describe the symptoms, but often I am able to sense the nature of the trouble before being told because it is replicated in my own body. To take two typical examples. I was able to tell that an injury to a man's foot was to the top of the foot rather than to the toes, before I had met the person concerned. I knew this from the feelings in my own foot.

Ministering to his wife, who had sinus trouble, my own nose blocked when I touched her face.

Sometimes the patient feels a great heat, or coldness where nerve treatment is being given. Often the hands vibrate over the area of the patient which requires the healing. Throughout I am guided by God, the Holy Spirit, and so I know when the vibrations cease that it is time to move to another location or to end the session. Sometimes I hear the Spirit saying interiorly, "Stop" or "That's it", and I know that the healing process is completed. At other times the process reaches its logical conclusion and it is obviously time to stop.

For instance, I was addressing a meeting in a rather gloomy room in Chesterfield when I noticed a woman called Sheila. She had previously asked for healing but we had never got round to it, for one reason or another. At the end of the meeting I called to her and she came out rather shyly and reluctantly. As I laid hands on her this rather superior lady began to sob uncontrollably, to everybody's surprise. She pulled off the scarf around her neck revealing a surgical collar crying out, "My neck, my neck". Suddenly that dreary room was filled by what I can only describe as the power of the Holy Spirit itself, and under my hands I felt the bones of her neck go click, clickety, click, click.

She wrote to me later, "You took me completely by surprise and I was intent on not disgracing myself in front of complete strangers. The power was so strong that I was overcome by the warmth and joy of His presence. That it should have happened to such an insignificant person as myself has left me with a glow inwardly as well as physically."

Sheila did not replace the collar after her healing. She quite rightly felt obliged to report the whole affair to her doctor, who asked if she had any pain. "No", she replied. "Well," he said, "if you have no pain you have no need of the collar. Just do away with it and be thankful for your healing."

George Bennett, in his book, *The Art of Healing*, ponders the relationship between medicine and healing. His conclusion is that while medicine is applied to the cure of disease, healing is concerned with the whole personality. Sheila had been treated for pain in her neck; the practical solution of the collar had been applied but the basis of her illness lay deeper than that.

When I first knew her husband he was one of the top men in a company in Chesterfield. During my time there the three top men were sacked or retired from their posts. One died shortly afterwards of a heart attack. One developed cancer, and Sheila's husband had a massive stroke, which had effectively made her his personal nurse for some years prior to her healing. She had to forget herself and her own pain, and give all her attention to looking after him. I suppose if the Church of England made saints Sheila would have been one of them.

These experiences are commonplace to me, and indeed some are shared by those who join with me in the laying on of hands, even at a distance. For instance, if we are doing a telephone link-up session the helpers who are in contact with the patient often feel heat or pain in their hands. This vanishes when the hands are shaken vigorously. These sensations help to guide the hands to those positions where there is disharmony or disease – a kind of divine "feed back" mechanism.

Another example of a situation requiring both medicine and the Healing Ministry concerned an acquaintance I was asked to help in 1991. Although he had assisted many times at Healing Services, he had never asked for healing himself. Now he was diagnosed as having a tumour which had shown up in a scan. He was taken into hospital for surgery and I went to pray with him. The doctors decided that he should go home as the operation had to be postponed for some reason. I told his wife, "I'm glad. It will give us more time for healing." The prognosis was not good and the surgeon told his wife that he had about six months to live at best. It was arranged that he would go back into hospital the following Sunday.

The operation was performed – but it was discovered that there was no tumour, only an abcess. I believe that this change occurred because so many people prayed for him. During our Healing Service several people had come forward and asked for prayer, not for themselves, but for their friend.

After the operation I went to the hospital to administer healing. Our friend was on an antibiotic drip and the outlook was still not optimistic. His wife was told that they expected him to be in hospital for some time. I visited daily for healing, and on the third day was surprised to hear that he was considered well enough to go home. However, my visit was not for nothing. His wife told me, "I wish you would do the healing because he so looks forward to it. It is something that he doesn't want to miss." I had been unaware of his feelings on the subject and it was lovely to hear these words. I laid hands on him. He packed his bags and went off home.

Perhaps our most promising advance in clergy/medical co-operation concerned a consultant surgeon in Sheffield. He began to help me with the laying on of hands during the Healing Services. He went off on a retreat where he heard God speaking directly to him, something a humanist psychiatrist might find strange and perhaps unhealthy. As a result of that encounter with God he felt called to full-time service in the Church, almost identical to the call I received twenty years ago, also at a retreat. Clearly such gatherings should be treated with respect and caution.

He gave up his post as consultant, with all the status and financial rewards that went with it, and is at present in training in the College of the Resurrection in West Yorkshire. When he has qualified he will be equally acceptable to both professions and possibly a strong bridge between the two, which is certainly needed. For instance, in chapter four there is an account of the healing of the boy John, paralysed due to an accident on the rugby field. It seemed sad, considering the outcome, that nobody in the hospital suggested that I might be useful in their spinal injuries unit, although they were aware of every detail of the case.

So far as I am concerned there is no conflict between medicine and healing. Medicine is obviously necessary. It is a wonderful gift from God; one of the various means He has established for restoring health. The administration of healing, the prayer, the lifting up of people to God are likewise means at His disposal. They add a dimension which medicine alone cannot give. Medicine cannot heal the spirit and it does nothing for the doctor, but the healer sees the love of God in action and is himself healed.

We are all going to die. There is a limit to the workings of both medicine and healing. This body is merely clay and is disposable, but the soul, the image of God who heals us if we let Him, lives in Eternity, in which this present life is but an episode. Some of us have discovered, or re-discovered, that we have a healing God, and the spread of this knowledge will revive the churches and supply them with a new dynamic.

We are learning that surgeons and chaplains, Church and medicine, can work together for the good of the whole person, and that with drugs and with prayer, things happen which would not happen without drugs or without prayer — a re-discovery of the unity of medicine, healing and the Church in our own day and time.

Chapter Nine

THE LAWS OF HEALING

Anyone who has read thus far will know that I am no academic theologian. In my Father's house there are many ministries and my calling was to a discipline where the teaching is by doing.

However, I would like to draw some conclusions, and perhaps issue a warning or two, from my experiences, if only to provide a starting point for those who follow. Obviously, while each healer will have preferences, there are no absolutes.

The word "laws" is probably misleading. There are no laws of the scientific or mathematical kind but there are a number of basic truths which are backed up by the experience of those who seriously pursue the Healing Ministry.

If asked, each might produce a somewhat different list of such truths, but they would overlap to give a large area of common ground. Perhaps you should make your own list, in which case the following points, or some of them, might become your own.

124

1. Christ is the Healer whether operating through the efforts of doctors and nurses or through the Power of the Holy Spirit.

The healer, by surrendering himself or herself to God, and by making himself or herself conscious of the Divine Power within, is enabled to take part in God's creative or recreative presence and activity. In certain cases the Power of God works in a most wonderful way, and we call them miracles. I've described the healing of Alice Jones as a coming together of earth and heaven. Although we know that Jesus by his incarnation joined together earth and heaven, these miracles are, in my own experience, quite few. One essential feature of those cases which may be deemed "successful" is, as we have already seen, faith, be it that of the sufferer, the friend or relative, or the worshipping community.

Often this faith is the faith of the mother. You will have read in this book of young men who have been involved in accidents and, in my view, it was the faith of the mother which in some way released the energizing love of God which enabled the patient to recover, often in a spectacular way.

2. Christ's injunction to His followers was two-fold: to preach the Gospel and to heal the sick.

The Gospel message was the more important. The principal function of the healing was to support the message which thus could not be easily ignored. It was for this that He came.

3. This injunction applied equally to His followers in all generations, not only to the original disciples and His immediate associates.
All were to have a part in the healing process.

4. Only the Holy Spirit can develop your capacity for healing and only in those who are willing to be possessed by Him.
It is not so much a gift as a capacity which can be developed by the Holy Spirit. You must be prepared to practise regularly and in a disciplined manner the consciousness of the Divine Presence, perhaps by setting aside a time such as Peddie's nightly "hour of watch".

I try to do at least two hours of meditation each day, resting in the love and power and energy of God, so that when the call comes, when the telephone call is made, or when I have to go and heal someone in the house, or in the church, God is able to work through me by the Power of God, the Holy Spirit. We have to be surrendered to God and available to our fellow human beings at one and the same time.

I believe that when we do co-operate with the creative love of God in His universe, somehow at that moment we become sons and daughters of God. Jesus took our humanity to give us His Divinity; and the Holy Spirit highlights the image of God in each of us.

5. The three modes of operation of the Divine Healing Power.

Cameron Peddie wrote in his book (Ref. 5) that he had a theory that the Divine Healing Power does three things. First it enables the patient to derive more benefit from the doctor's treatment than would otherwise happen. Second, it helps to set the natural healing powers of the body in operation. Third, if anything more is required then the Divine Power is capable of supplying whatever may be needed.

If nothing is required then nothing is given. The merely curious are bound to be disappointed.

6. The Mechanics of Healing

It is generally agreed that prayer plus the laying on of hands seems to be more effective than prayer alone. It is the method most often used by Jesus.

Still more effective is prayer plus the placing of hands on the affected area of the patient. This is not to infer that intercessory prayer is of a lower order in the scale of things. Prayer is our greatest privilege – the basic preparation for our hearts and minds – but the laying on of hands seems to be more focused and specific. In Matthew's Gospel we read that Jesus touched the eyes of two blind men and at once they were able to see. He did not simply hold a consultation with them. Just as he heard their cry over the noise of the crowd, however, we can be sure He still hears our prayer. No one, however obscure, feeble or disabled, should think that they can have no influence on events in the world, great or small, so long as they can pray.

7. The Limits of Proof

Arguably the most important question every one of us has to confront is whether or not God exists and, if so, what we should do about it. Anything by way of a miraculous happening grabs everybody's attention. What does this mean, we ask ourselves? Can we say that because a large ulcer disappears suddenly, not even leaving a mark, therefore God exists since no other agency could do such a thing? Suppose we multiply this by a thousand such incidents, do we thereby force the great mass of unbelievers to their knees?

Obviously not. God will not compel us to enter the Kingdom of Heaven. We have to choose to follow Him, and for that we must have the freedom to choose not to follow Him. So there will always be an escape route available for those who decide to go that way; to rationalize rather than to pay the high cost of belief which includes changing our lifestyle. The cost was too high for the rich young ruler of the gospel and it is still too high for many, rich or poor.

The American healer and writer, C. Peter Wagner (Ref. 1), put it this way, "If people believe that God does not heal today, they will not be able to see (i.e. recognize) divine healing, no matter what quantity of documentation or proof is provided." Jesus said that even if someone rose from the dead the sceptics would not be persuaded, and He refused to give them the "sign" they asked for (Luke 16:31).

On the other hand, experience shows that when people who are fair-minded witness for themselves the power of the Holy Spirit, then faith is born or their belief is magnified. This is not some faint echo from heavenly places of events far distant in time. This is God in the living room; in the place of work; everywhere. They are often heard to say that whatever healing of their bodies they may have received is secondary to this great discovery.

8. Success and Failure: The Two Imposters

The results are not, I think, our concern. The relationship between God and each individual soul is their own business. All we have to do is to fulfil the need which is before us at the moment. The outcome, whether healing or cure, belongs to God alone.

Here I have to part company with the American healer C. Peter Wagner. He is a great believer in "accountability" (Ref. 10). In his view, groups or churches that have gained a public reputation for a healing ministry should keep track of their results, and make this information public. When he prays for a person he gives them a report form which they return to him when enough time has elapsed for them to know whether something has happened or not. His results for 114 forms for 1987 were:

No improvement	18%
Some improvement	28%
Considerable improvement	25%
Completely well	29%

Wagner also quotes results of a group known to him of 325 trained lay people in 80 prayer teams called the Vineyard Christian Fellowship of Anaheim, California. The results for 600 cases in 1987 are almost identical to his own.

No improvement	19%
Some or considerable improvement	58%
Completely well	26%

In both cases over 80 per cent recorded some improvement, which is surely impressive.

While I have no plans to set up such a system it is encouraging to get feed back from time to time. For instance, the other day I was entertaining friends to lunch at a remote inn outside Sheffield, deep in the moors, when a young man of about nineteen years of age came to the table. He had been cooking in the kitchen and recognized my voice. Without preamble he informed us that I had been the one who had been involved in getting rid of his brain tumour five years earlier.

Although this sort of thing happens quite often, there are many occasions when there is no reporting back, either good or bad, and I have to remind myself that results are not my concern.

Peddie said there are no complete failures, and I believe that is true. I think everybody receives something, although maybe not the sort of physical healing that they expect. I agree with him that illnesses are often deep-seated and consequently in need of "deep" healing. When I am lecturing to the clergy I often say that it is not what our bodies have done to us, but what we have done to our bodies that is the trouble. For example some healers, including myself, are strongly of the view that arthritis has its origins in long-term resentment in the patient. To be cured, the resentment has to be eliminated.

This is true of other complaints too. Where there is an underlying cause, perhaps emotional, it must be dealt with first. Perhaps someone from the patient's past must be forgiven, or the patient has committed some sin which he cannot be rid of and which has become an irritant, finding physical expression in some illness. The symptoms may readily respond to healing, but the cause remains potent. In this respect I have to disagree with Cameron Peddie. He states that in his experience with rheumatic cases (p. 55) every type does yield but it requires time and patience. He adds that rheumatoid arthritis, fibrosis, sciatica and lumbago respond fairly quickly, but osteo-arthritis and neuritis are very stubborn. Two to four months pass before the pain and restrictive movement in osteo-arthritis begin to disappear. I would agree that arthritis often responds rapidly with better movement and a decrease in swelling. However, this relief can be temporary and requires more sessions to sustain it. Some healers, including myself, are strongly of the view that the complaint has its origins in long-term resentment in the patient, as described here.

Should we therefore ask the patient to confess his sins and repent before giving a service of healing? Peddie says "no" (Ref. 12) and I agree. Confession and repentance should come after the service, when the patient has felt the power of God. Jesus only asked the patient by way of preparation, "Do you believe I can heal you?" That was all. There was no other preparation and no other conditions. When organizing a formal healing service, however, it would be logical to include confession and repentance in the order of service a shown in Appendix 2.

Sometimes illness is necessary for us, and we can be reluctant to give it up. We think we have a cold, or perhaps we are "run down". We don't know whether it is in fact really a cold or whether we are simply fed up with our situation. With our illness we are able to go back into the womb and be comfortable and content. So not only must the healer surrender to the creative love of God, but also the person coming for healing.

9. The nature of the healing power
In his book *The Forgotten Talent* (Ref. 2) the Revd J. Cameron Peddie discussed the specific nature of the power which operates in the Healing Ministry.

He points out that while He was present with His disciples our Lord was able to impart the necessary power to them by which they could heal all manner of sickness. Before He left He told them that henceforth the arrangements for making power available would be changed. It would be distributed by an agency He called the Holy Ghost. This power would be everywhere available at all times and places.

Notice that the disciples were not simply given a licence to cure. They were to be the custodians of a power to be used in their principal function of witnessing for Him. This power would be separate from the Holy Spirit, the distributor.

It is this power we are dealing with in the Healing Ministry, and according to Peddie it is mediated by Jesus who "adapts the volume of Divine Grace to the need and receptive powers of the patient". He supports this view by his experiences of the laying on of hands when he has observed that the volume of power gradually increases in strength and, when enough has been ministered, decreases until it is completely withdrawn. All of this is in accord with my own experiences. Occasionally when I am laying hands on a patient I am aware of another hand on mine and I can feel that it is the pierced hand of the Risen Christ.

What more can we learn of this power?

Reading the gospels one is drawn to the fact that Jesus did not accomplish His healing miracles by a snap of His fingers, like some magician. He seems to be possessed of some kind of energy which He directs by laying His hands on the patients or, as in the case of the centurion's servant, by radiation over a distance. Where the trouble was of a nervous origin He would merely speak to the sufferer.

All of this suggests some sort of electro-magnetic energy, and it would seem that the same sort of thing is manifest in those who offer themselves for healing work today.

Of all the healers I have met or read about J. Cameron Peddie must be the most practical and analytical. It is as if he sees the healing forces as another area of God's natural phenomena, as yet unexplained but as real as all the others (Ref. 3). He writes:

I have ministered to several scientists and from what they experienced under such services, they all agree that the operative principle in the ministry is the radiation principle; that by surrender to the Divine Power for cleansing and sanctification we become receiving and transmitting instruments of a healing "ray". From the strange sense of activity that goes on in the frontal lobes of my brain during a service, a sense of activity that is most intense about the middle of the forehead, I would even say that some of my brain cells act as receiving and transmitting valves for the divine "rays" of healing love and grace. The learned may say that in so thinking and speaking I am reducing what is purely spiritual to the level of the material. Quite the opposite; I am raising the material to the level of the spiritual. In the last analysis this material creation of God is fundamentally spiritual. We now approach the conclusion of the whole matter. It is this. This ministry of Divine Healing really is a science conceived and made possible by the only comprehensive and unerring scientist in existence – the Divine Creator. By His foresight and planning and creative power He made wireless, television and all the other thrilling aspects of modern civilization possible. But He also devised, planned and created an instrument, the human personality, capable of "tuning in" for personal benefit, to the rays of His redeeming love. Thus it is able to pick up the healing rays that radiate from His throne and transmit them to all in need.

Light is also a form of energy. I have described in chapter five, "Healing in Public", how, when I begin to heal, it is as if I am stepping into a column of pure white light which extends about a foot in front of my body. Peddie also describes a vision of light when treating his first patient thus:

The patient was covered with blankets. But I saw her lying in a bath of golden light so indescribable in its beauty and brilliance, I can only call it the glory of God. She lay in that light during the whole half hour I was ministering and I felt God was thus making clear to me the reality of His presence and power.

As Dr C. Peter Wagner (Ref. 4), the American writer, might have put it, "Believing is seeing".

Another example of unexplained energy occurred when another Church of Scotland minister, the Revd Allan Old, was administering healing to a lady who was suffering from cancer. His account of the incident is as follows:

> While we were in Canada we experienced a good illustration of how God uses several methods to bring about His purposes. Late one afternoon I got a phone call to go down to the General Hospital as the mother of one of my members was critically ill there. I knew this lady had cancer. When I got to the hospital I found this patient was now in intensive care, and was heavily sedated. I don't know why I checked the time as I went in, but I must have done so as I remember the time was 5.27 pm. My verbal prayer was brief as I did not know if the patient was really able to take in what I was saying, but I sat until a few minutes to six in silent prayer holding a hand of the patient. At that time the anaesthetist came in, and asked if I minded if they now examined the patient, because

if she were strong enough, which she had not been until this time, they must try to do an operation. It seemed that without this operation the expectancy of life would be three to four days. I went off home but got a phone call from the family about 9.30 pm. Mother had had the operation and was doing well, but at what time had I visited her? I reported my visit had been from just before 5.30 pm until just before 6 pm. "Well, we've just been told that some of the apparatus which had been hooked up to Mother showed a remarkable surge of power between 5.30 and 6 pm and that is why the surgeon was able to operate." The patient did well, got home shortly, and is alive and well today, about fifteen years after. But one of the most interesting things about this is a remark the surgeon made to the patient shortly before she got home. "Ah, you are the lady who should not be alive. It was not what we did that saved your life, it must have been power from above (pointing upwards)". He was of course a Christian doctor, and an excellent surgeon.

The instances given above are typical of many similar examples pointing to the presence, during healing, of some special form of energy.

In a closely packed crowd Jesus sensed the healing of the woman who touched His robe. Did He not feel a discharge of this energy and, when He went off alone in the desert, was He not "recharging" from some private resource?

In a recent case in Rotherham Hospital, I went to see a young man who had been in intensive care following an accident. His eyes were covered with gauze and he was completely immobile. When I laid my hands on his head it was just as though we were kick-starting one of those old cars that we used to run forty years ago.

... AND A FINAL THOUGHT

Clearly, Divine Healing is never likely to become an overcrowded profession. This is one of the most intractable problems. Unless the clergy take up this ministry in earnest we cannot avoid disappointing great masses of people, simply due to there being insufficient hours in the day to treat them all, particularly as many require multiple treatments.

You will not find all the answers in this book, but Jesus Himself is the answer to all man's questions concerning the Father and His laws. Know Him and that is all one needs to know. His is the only power we have to bring to bear, and we can only expect to exercise this power if we obey His well-documented commands.

Healing the sick was His idea. It supports the preaching of the Word like nothing else can. The rewards include a deeper, more vital and authoritative ministry.

We cannot ignore it and still call ourselves servants of the Most High.

Appendix One

A PIONEER
AND HIS METHODS

It will now be obvious that the Revd J. Cameron Peddie has been a major influence and inspiration in my career.

To appreciate the scale of his achievements we have to examine his circumstances. He was ordained to the ministry in 1917 to the linked charge of Kennoway and Windygates of the United Free Church. Both churches were in decline but within three years he had so improved their situation that each could merit a minister. He resigned, intending to become a doctor, but while he waited for the course to begin at Aberdeen University he received a call from a local church and could not refuse. He felt that God had a special task for him to do. So he found himself in the Glasgow Gorbals, one of the most deprived areas of the city, the charge being the amalgamation of three churches, namely Cuninghame, the Old Briggate Parish and Hutchesontown Parish. Today all these churches have been swept away and the area rebuilt but there are still some of his parishioners alive who remember him with affection.

The united Hutchesontown Parish seems to have been a happy place with all the usual organisations full to overflowing; the youth organisations were particularly successful. It was not all deadly serious – there was a social side to the many activities, with dances as well as district visiting.

Peddie might have been remembered simply as a particularly effective parish minister had it not been for the infamous gangs of the 1930s. It was a time of high unemployment. There were about thirty of these gangs, each consisting of up to 200 youngsters. They terrorised the shop keepers and were involved in all kinds of petty crime and even murder during their street battles for supremancy; a bit like West Side Story without the music.

The parents begged their minister to do something about it and he resolved to tackle the problem. The story is well-known in Glasgow of how the thirty gangs became thirty boys' clubs and useful work was found or created for idle hands to do. What is less well-known is the way Cameron Peddie went about it. A brave man might have gone and preached the Gospel to the gangs. Instead he chose to do what he imagined Jesus would have done. It happened to be that time of the year when he took his annual holiday of one month. He decided to spend this month, with no mention of religion, simply mixing with these young gangsters, being with them and treating them as Jesus might have done, starting with the top gang. The transformation began from there.

This gives us the key to the character of the man. His approach to every task was to do it as Jesus might have done, whatever the odds stacked against him. This made him the ideal choice to initiate the healing ministry in Scotland. A lesser man might have said "Who am I to disagree with the official line of the distinguished theologians?" By contrast I had the encouragement of bishops. Another might say "I am only one minister in two thousand, many of whom are senior to me. Why should they pay any attention to me?" Yet another might say "How would I go about it? I wouldn't know how to start", whereas I inherited the knowledge and teaching of Mary Rogers; and a great many might say, "That is all very well, but I have a hundred things more pressing to do with my time than to speculate on doctrine. Surely that is for the academics!" He must have been aware of all this but nothing was allowed to deflect him from his purpose. Once he was sure of his calling he simply went ahead, totally unabashed at the enormity of what he was doing. He had his orders and he knew his Jesus.

In time many would follow his example – and that would take courage – but initially he was on his own, waiting for years for his commission from God. Established churches must be amongst the most conservative of organizations, suspicious of change and not easily moved to admission that there might be something lacking in their basic beliefs and practices. As a Divinity student he had been taught that the injunction "Preach the Gospel, heal the sick" applied only to the disciples and their immediate followers, so far as healing the sick was concerned, not to any "latter day" disciples (Ref. 7). As he waited, year after year, he must have wondered whether his teachers were right after all.

Against this background Cameron Peddie worked out his own theology, always a thorny path to tread; established his own procedures for confronting sickness and human frailty in all their variety; and instructed those brave souls who followed his example.

Peddie is careful to stress in *The Forgotten Talent* that the purpose of the signs and wonders is to confirm the words of preaching (Ref. 9), as illustrated in Mark's gospel, where we read "The disciples went everywhere preaching the word *with signs following*" (Mark 16:20).

Particularly noteworthy among his methods was his discipline of the nightly hour with God from eleven to midnight, obviously his means of developing his acute sense of the Divine Presence, which he counted as being particularly important for those who wish to do special work for the Lord.

Likewise, the offering of himself in every aspect; physical, mental and spiritual for this work. Notwithstanding all this, it still took five years before God gave him the sign he sought, and that was given thirty years to the day after his ordination.

After Peddie's death in 1968 the Revd F. A. Smith wrote the following appreciation of the man and his methods.

A great life on this earth has come to an end, but because God never wasted any good thing, the influence of Cameron Peddie still remains and we can be sure that he is moving on at this moment to some new experience of the love of God in the life beyond.

I don't think Cameron Peddie would like that first phrase, for he was essentially a humble man. Yet those of us who knew him through the years have no hesitation in ascribing greatness to him. He would, quite rightly, give all the credit for any success to his Saviour Jesus Christ. Yet, in his discipleship, Cameron Peddie was great.

When I first met him and learned something of his inner life, what impressed me, and to my mind gave him a genuine authority, was the fact that every night from eleven to twelve midnight he kept a spiritual vigil with his God. He spoke from an intimacy with God that few men have ever possessed. Yet he never at any moment forgot he was ministering to men and women and little children on this earth. He knew he served a God who was concerned with the bodies and minds as well as the eternal souls of men and women. He sought to do what he believed his Lord commanded him to do – preach the Gospel and heal the sick, and many are those who benefited because of his obedience.

I do not need to repeat what he himself has revealed about his life in the book *The Forgotten Talent*. But I can give some information about his influence on the development of healing within the Church of Scotland. The ministers who gathered around Cameron Peddie in the group which met in Community House in the early 1950s soon realized that he was their real inspiration. He led them to begin Intercessory Groups and to practise the "laying on of hands" among their people. Most strongly he emphasized that this ministry should be part of every minister's work. No one was cut off from it. The command of our Lord to heal the sick was just as clearly given to every minister as was the command to preach the Gospel. So sure was he of this that he accompanied most of the ministers at one time or another to a sick person, ministered to them, but insisted that the minister himself should share in the Healing Service. After one or two visits Cameron Peddie would say to the minister, "Now, carry on yourself. It is your work as well as mine. You must do as I do in the grace of the Lord Jesus." So the work spread, for none could deny his challenge.

The extent of his work was little realized. He travelled at times hundreds of miles in response to a call. And his own clinic was over busy with those needing help.

Most of the ministers who joined the Glasgow Group followed the lead given by Cameron Peddie. For him the laying on of hands was more than a momentary gesture. Often he would spend up to half an hour praying, laying his hands in silence, stimulating the trust of the sick person, talking with them about themselves and establishing a genuine caring relationship with them. He always finished by moving his hands from head to toe, just above the surface of the body, with successive sweep

147

of the hands to give the final blessing. This action had a surprising effect. It stimulated as if sea breezes were blowing new life into the stricken body. This ministration seemed to be particularly his own idea.

I should like to record also our great appreciation to Mrs Peddie who, through the years, supported her husband faithfully in all his many labours. We record how much the healing movement owes to her for her work behind the scenes.

The Revd Fred A. Smith — Westerton

The Revd Allan Old, who has pursued the Healing Ministry in the USA and Canada as well as in Britain, records this first-hand account of healing by Cameron Peddie:

About this time, in course of preparation for our evening worship, I came across an article in a paper about the Revd J. Cameron Peddie, a Glasgow minister now semi-retired, who had done remarkable work in the ministry of Divine Healing. I did not know Mr Peddie as he was a member of a different Presbytery and lived in the city of Glasgow, while we were quite a number of miles away in the suburbs. I had a physical problem which the orthopaedic surgeon could not help, and I wondered if Mr Peddie might be able to do something for me. (My problem resulted from a fall on Ben Nevis when trying to help a girl who had got into difficulties. A milogram examination in North America had injured some nerves in my spine). I contacted Mr Peddie, who in his retirement was living at Cumbernauld. He invited me to visit and so that he could give me what he called a service. Having read his book *The Forgotten Talent* I was prepared for what he would do.

After we had had a friendly chat he settled me in a chair then stood in front of me about two feet away. He then raised both hands level with my head and slowly lowered them, never touching me but only two or three inches from the surface of my face or clothes. He did this several times quite slowly then placed both hands on my back and prayed followed by a period of silent prayer. The interesting thing was that as he very slowly lowered his hands in front of me a fresh breeze seemed to come from them. (My wife Isobel who was sitting fifteen or twenty feet away felt this also.) Mr Peddie's daughter used to call this "Daddy's sea breezes". And the breeze had a fragrance, my wife and I thought to be very similar to that of a pine wood. This fragrance came from small beads of oil which appeared on the palms of his hands after Mr Peddie started to work.

I don't know how many services I had from Mr Peddie over the next few months, but I know my back was improving when Mr Peddie turned ill and shortly died. He is the only person, and I have had laying on of hands from several of the world's best known healers, but he is the only person who has been able to help my back at all. If he had lived a little longer it seemed as if the back would have been healed. It seemed that God's Holy Spirit was able to flow through him in a remarkable way. Anyay, though I was not fully healed Isobel and I greatly enjoyed our contact with Mr Peddie and his wife. One day I asked him if he would be willing to sign a few copies of the prayer he often used during his Healing Service and I still have one of these pasted into his book *The Forgotten Talent*.

After he died his wife kindly brought the wooden cross he had had in his sanctuary to me. If I were asked what were my lasting impressions of this man of God I would say his kindliness and his humility. I have always been surprised and sorry that he received no special recognition, from either church or city, for his work amongst the gangs of the 1930s, or his Healing Ministry.

I am grateful to Mr Old for a signed copy of the prayer mentioned above, written by Cameron Peddie wrote for the use of the patient:

Special Prayer for Healing
Father of all health and healing, Redeemer of body, mind and soul, a helpless suppliant I come to Thee. The hand of man faileth me; but Thy hand cannot fail. The word of man proves powerless to release me from my affliction; but Thy word has still its ancient power. I thank Thee for all that man has attempted but failed to do on my behalf. Now I wait on Thy triumphant Love and Power. Mighty Redeemer, manifest Thy glory in my healing, Thy Truth in my restoration through Thy Son Jesus Christ, my Lord.

AMEN

Once a person is captivated by the Healing Ministry there is no turning back. For instance, Mr Old came to the testing time when he felt he had to tell his congregation of his new discovery. He writes:

In the month of December 1964 I decided to tell my congregation something about this experience, at a morning service, and from now on when I had prayer with the sick I would lay on hands and seek God's special blessing and healing for the sick person. I felt that in honesty this for a time would be experimental, as I could promise blessing from God but I could not promise healing. My people were surprisingly sympathetic and co-operative. If any disagreed with what I was doing, they did not tell me, and the result was that we began to see healings, confirmed by doctors as very unexpected.

The numbers attending our evening services were not large, so our Session agreed to change these services into times of Bible study, prayer and discussion on the Healing Ministry of Christ and the similar work being done in His name today. I was delighted and surprised to find a new joy and new power developing in my ministry, and noticed too that this happened in a quiet, reverent way. My one fear in the Charismatic Movement had been that over-emotionalism might develop, as I had sometimes come across this in various places in both Britain and North America. I need not have worried, we were still able to express our worship in peace and with reverence, though a new meaningfulness and vitality flowed in.

On one of my rare visits to Scotland Mr Old introduced me to the Eric Liddell Church Centre at 15 Morningside Road, Edinburgh; this area being known locally as "Holy Corner", on account of the number of impressive church buildings crowded together. This Centre is a powerhouse of the Healing Ministry and a meeting place of the Christian Fellowship of Healing (Scotland). I mention it particularly because of their excellent selection of leaflets describing this ministry. They are well worth acquiring. They are brief, accurate and inspirational, bringing together the essentials in an easily assimilated form. The Fellowship of Healing is interdenominational, as also is the Fellowship of Meditation mentioned earlier.

It was interesting to learn from Mr Old that the Church of Scotland has had an "official" interest in Divine Healing for a good many years. The Board of Social Responsibility has a sub-committee, known as the Committee on Health and Healing. In the Annual Report to the General Assembly in 1992, this committee reports a growing interest in healing as part of the Church's normal worship, witness and activity. The report also states that in April 1991 thirty ministers who have their own Ministries of Healing met in Glasgow, and that in October 1991 the Healing Conference held at Carberry Tower was over subscribed by forty applications. Consideration is being given to having an extra conference at Carberry Tower this year. The Church of Scotland continues to be a member of the London-based Churches' Council for Health and Healing.

Appendix Two

SERVICE OF BENEDICTION AND HEALING

St Matthew's Church
Carver Street, Sheffield

Exposition KNEEL
After the Blessed Sacrament has been placed on the altar we sing O Salutaris.

O saving Victim! opening wide
The gate of Heaven to man below
Our foes press hard on every side –
Thine aid supply, thy strength bestow.

All praise and thanks to thee ascend
For evermore, blest One in Three;
O grant us life that shall not end
In our true native land with thee. Amen.

Prayers
Priest: Blessed, praised, hallowed and adored be Jesus Christ on his throne of glory.

All: And in the most holy Sacrament of the Altar.

Hymn STAND
The monstrance is veiled during this hymn.

155

Scripture Reading SIT

Address

Act of Repentance KNEEL

Priest: My brothers and sisters, to prepare ourselves for this ministry of healing let us call to mind our sins.

All: I confess to almighty God, and to you, my brothers and sisters, that I have sinned through my own fault, in my thoughts and in my words, in what I have done, and in what I have failed to do; and I ask Blessed Mary ever Virgin, all the angels and saints, and you, my brothers and sisters, to pray for me to the Lord our God.

Priest: May almighty God have mercy on us, forgive us our sins, and bring us to everlasting life.

All: Amen.

Laying on of Hands and Anointing SIT

[If you wish to receive this Sacrament of Healing for yourself or on behalf of someone else please come up to the communion step. If preferred, you can remember the names and needs of others, and your own needs, silently before God.]

Hymn STAND

The Monstrance is Unveiled KNEEL

Kneeling again before the Blessed Sacrament, we sing Tantum Ergo.

Therefore we, before him bending,
This great Sacrament revere;
Types and shadows have their ending,
For the newer rite is here;

156

Faith, our outward sense befriending,
Makes the inward vision clear.

Glory let us give and blessing
To the Father and the Son;
Honour, might and praise addressing,
While eternal ages run;
Ever too his love confessing,
Who, from both, with both is one. Amen

Priest: Thou gavest them Bread from Heaven. Alleluia!
All: Containing in itself all sweetness. Alleluia!

Collect

O God, Who in a wonderful Sacrament hast left unto us the
Memorial of Thy Passion: Grant us, we beseech Thee, so to
venerate the Sacred Mysteries of Thy Body and Blood that
we may ever perceive within ourselves the fruit of Thy
Redemption; Who livest and reignest, world without end.
Amen.

Benediction

*All worship Our Lord in silence as He blesses us when the
sign of the Cross is made with the Blessed Sacrament. The
bell rings to call us to adoration.*

The Divine Praises
Each repeated after the priest.

Blessed be God
Blessed be His Holy Name
Blessed be Jesus Christ, true God and true Man
Blessed be the name of Jesus
Blessed be His most sacred Heart
Blessed be his most Precious Blood
Blessed be Jesus in the Most Holy Sacrament of the Altar
Blessed be the Holy Spirit, the Comforter

Blessed be the great Mother of God, Mary most Holy
Blessed be her holy and immaculate Conception
Blessed be her glorious Assumption
Blessed be the name of Mary, Virgin and Mother
Blessed be Saint Joseph, her Spouse most chaste
Blessed be God in His Angels and in His Saints

The Blessed Sacrament is
Returned to the Aumbry

Hymn   STAND

NOTES

The Forgotten Talent: God's Ministry of Healing,
  J. Cameron Peddie. Originally published in
  Great Britain in 1961 by the Oldbourne Book
  Co. Ltd; then issued as a Fontana Paperback in
  1966; currently published by Arthur James,
  London (ISBN 0 85305 266 2)

References: 2: p. 119   7: p. 13
              3: p. 123   9: p. 14
              5: p. 54   11: p. 55
              6: p. 88   12: p. 73

*How to Have a Healing Ministry without Making
  Your Church Sick*, C. Peter Wagner. Monarch
  Publications, 1988 (ISBN 1 85424 050 1)

References: 1: p. 143
              4: p. 142
              8: p. 208
             10: p. 243